Praise for Daughter of the Border . . .

"*Daughter of the Border*, Roberta Hamburgh's debut family memoir of three generations of exceptional women of the West and Southwest, is a stunning tribute to the courage she and the women of her family exhibited in the face of challenging situations and multicultural divides. Readers who hunger for breathtaking stories of strong women and the old (and new) West will devour this book, all the while eagerly looking forward to whatever this oh-so-talented and insightful author writes next." — Rosemary Daniell, award-winning author of *Secrets of the Zona Rosa: How Writing (and Sisterhood) Can Change Women's Lives*

"Exquisite! This book takes us on an important journey across boundaries and back again. It is a tender and living exploration of what it means to be a woman, a girl, a daughter and a human in our complicated world." — Molly Caro May, author of *The Map of Enough: One Woman's Search for Place*

Daughter of the Border

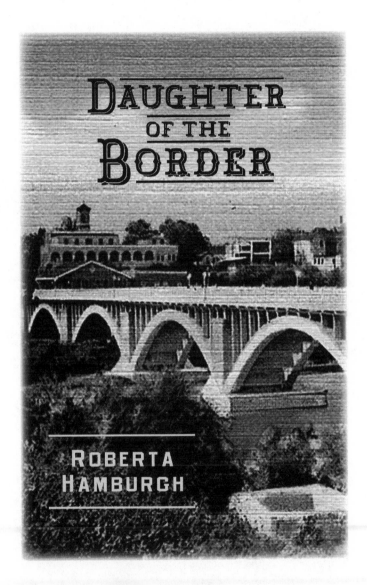

DAUGHTER
OF THE
BORDER

ROBERTA
HAMBURGH

Bink Books

Bedazzled Ink Publishing Company • Fairfield, California

978-1-945805-69-1 paperback

Bink Books
a division of
Bedazzled Ink Publishing Company
Fairfield, California
http://www.bedazzledink.com

Acknowledgements

My parents, Robert and Roseglen, allowed me to grow up in South Texas near Mexico giving me a gift of a border homeland. And my love, Harvey Hamburgh inspires and encourages my writing each day as does my sister, Rita Lockhart, teacher extraordinaire, who gave me freedom by telling me I could write anything about our lives that I wished to include. My daughter Monica also encourages me in my writing endeavors. My two writing teachers, Rosemary Daniell of Savannah, Georgia and Molly May of Bozeman, Montana, guided me all the way through with knowledge and kindness. My Second Mother, Mary Willie Billie Shannon Muth McKinley, read it all and encouraged my writing as did her daughter and my friend, Elaine McKinley. Francis Taylor and Iris Bibliowitz also read and edited, and my friend Suzanne Christopher read and commented on the whole rough draft. Nonnie Hughes, Linda Babcock and Meta Newhouse are my main book reveal cheerleaders! And artist Rossella Vasta encouraged me when I did some of my writing at her villa in Tuscany. Alberto Braccini greatly encouraged me while I wrote on the patio area of the Firenze Public Library in Italy. And finally a big thank-you to my editor, C.A. Casey.

And under everything a liquid from way below the stuff of fossils, liquefied, spread out and deep into the earth. This was the beginning of all our family. It underlay everything and its greasiness and dirt crept into the corners of all of our lives.

One

The Brothers
1909

RETA LAY ON the feather bed, traveling clothes on, eyes wide open, staring at the pink paisley wallpaper. She stared until it blurred and her eyes watered.

Was today the last day she'd see Blind Boone? The last time she'd hear him make his piano imitate a banjo, a fiddle, guitar, or even a fife and drum? She'd been seven years old when she'd first gone to downtown Nebraska City to the ice cream parlor where Boone played on Saturdays. That day they'd ridden on a horse wagon—she holding her father's hand tight as he held on to the leather strap for passengers to steady themselves for the ride. Today they'd gone down in a streetcar, a more sophisticated form of transportation. She'd had a double scoop of ice cream while listening to Boone play the ragtime numbers her mother had told her he'd learned in St. Louis bordellos. The thought of bordellos flushed her adolescent cheeks. Today her mind had not been on his music, although she'd tried to pay attention so she'd have it in her head if she went through with the plan.

She heard a muffled conversation going on in the parlor down below. She imagined that Bob and William were telling her parents the specifics of the two brothers' scheme to go out to the Wyoming territory to drill for oil, to make their fortunes.

Nebraska City was a jumping-off point for people heading out west. Her father often let wanderers stay with the family for several days, as these brothers had done. He liked their stories and perhaps lived his pioneer streak through the visitors.

She was both terrified and thrilled, knowing that while Bob and William did have the plan they were describing, they also had an addition to that plan—to take her along. For William was to marry her as soon as they got to a place far enough away, where they could find a marrying preacher or a justice of the peace, and her family wouldn't be known.

She had no intention of letting someone alarm her parents with knowledge of the plan before it succeeded. She knew she was young to do this, only sixteen, but her father had always told her she was the brave daughter, braver than anyone else in the family. His believing that made her think she could be strong and actually follow this plan. This bravery was all she had from him.

Charles Franklin Sipple was a hardhearted man who chewed out her mother, Lenore, over the least failing in her constant work to keep her family in house and home. Reta wondered if her father had become so bloodless because he hadn't pursued the westward dream. She knew he once courted such from the long-into-the-night discussions he had with the adventurers who stayed with them before heading to the frontier. These men added to her mother's work and her father's heartache.

Now, with the two visitors, she would head for Wyoming to find that fortune. William had told her there were places out there where oil bubbles to the surface of pools of water.

"Indians," he'd said, "seine it off for war paints, decorating tepees, and liniments for what ails you. It's that easy to come by. We will drill for it. And when it comes, we will sell it for big money."

She was canny enough to know that the fortune might not materialize. Her father had come to Nebraska from Kentucky with such a plan, yet they now lived in a little house outside of Nebraska City. Charles Sipple still drove freight wagons he didn't own, and Lenore took in laundry to make ends meet.

Ethel, her younger sister by two years, stirred on the bed next to Reta.

William's older brother, Bob, had told her he'd never met a Reta and asked for the spelling, which also surprised him. She told him that her mother had wanted her to be unique and strong. She realized that now she had an opportunity to live up to that expectation. She wondered if Ethel was concerned to be left behind.

Reta and Ethel were a contrast in colors. Ethel had lush brown hair and olive skin, while Reta's luminous white skin was transparent, showing pulsing light blue veins. Her red hair drew compliments, and at times she seemed lit from within.

Earlier, when they sat on their bed brushing each other's long hair, she'd told her sister in whispers, "William, the younger one, wants to marry me. I see a certainty and willingness in his eyes. I want to leave this life of struggling in school and working laundry until bedtime. Boys who are freighters or butchers are our only choice here. But these Ingersoll brothers come from Pennsylvania where Bob studied art and William learned about oil drilling. They want a different life. A better life. And that's what I want."

"I didn't know you wanted that," Ethel said sniffling, her only response to Reta's soliloquy except for tear-filled eyes.

"My goodness, Ethel, the only valentine I got from a boy this year said, 'I never sausage eyes as thine, And if you'd butcher hand in mind, And liver round me every day, We'd seek some ham-let far away.'" She emphasized the meat words, and they both giggled and lay down, their arms wound tightly around each other as a goodbye.

"Now I realize why you're dressed," Ethel reported. "When are you going?"

"When mother and father and our brothers are soundly asleep. He truly wants me to go with him."

"And so you must . . ." Ethel managed a few minutes later. And as her eyes closed, she squeezed Reta hard.

First, she waited for Ethel to fall asleep; then for her parents and brothers to ascend the stairs and talk in muffled voices in their rooms; and, finally, a proper amount of silence. She got up quietly and pulled the filled carpetbag William had given her for luggage out from under the bed. She looked in the blurry mirror, brushing the loose strands back into a bun. Then she tiptoed down the stairs, bumping the carpetbag quietly, trying to keep her exit secret.

Out back by the horse barn, William and Bob were packing numerous bags into their horse-drawn wagon, and when she asked, they said in whispered voices that her dad had many too many clothes and tools for him to wear in his lifetime, so they'd borrowed a few.

"Your brothers helped us pick them out."

She made a mental note that now that she was going, she'd agreed to new rules. She looked back at the sad little house and climbed up into the wagon. As they trolled slowly down the silent road, she turned her head just once to look back at the house's shadow on the barn. She felt a twinge of sadness at leaving her mother and sister and brothers but none at leaving her father.

Her mother spent her long, hard days steeling herself so as to not to be much bothered by the cold, uncaring ways of her husband, instead concentrating on her offspring. What would they do when they waken and find her gone?

Riding between them on the buckboard gave her plenty of opportunity to size up the brothers. They rode through dust storms and rain, and as the light came on, she realized that although Bob might be the plodder, he was also the thinker. William shot his mouth off more often and without thinking. Although younger, William bossed Bob around. She saw him as domineering. "Are you watching the right side? That horse seems a bit lame."

Bob pointed out things to her in the landscape and gave her notice of sounds she could learn to identify. "We are driving in a gully now, not really a road but a washed-out river or creek bed that people have decided is the way to go. If the river went this way, it must be the path of least resistance. As we get closer to the Platte River, you'll hear the water calling out before you see it."

"Grab the blankets from the back, for god's sake—it's raining," William ordered.

"Over there is a ravine, a deep place in the earth, and if it is wide enough, homesteaders put their houses there to protect them from the dust and snow storms. The trees are red oak, and those are sand hills behind the bluffs of the Platte," Bob shared.

"Quit weaving your body back and forth. It tilts the wagon," William commanded her.

Before she'd experienced it, she'd never thought of dust as coming in a storm, and now she could feel its prickles in the raindrops on her arms from the previous day's duster. Something was constantly at her.

In the mornings, as the three of them lay side by side in the wagon bed, a cotton summer cover their only protection, she watched the morning light coming on. William commanded the middle place to give her a bit of privacy in sleep.

One morning, Bob pointed out that the beautiful repetitive sound, which had become their wake-up, was the call of the bobolink. "The sound that may haunt you in the night is old coyote." He was helping her to see details and to hear the beauty in the wide prairie they were crossing, through Nebraska and up from Cheyenne to their destination, Thermopolis, Wyoming.

One night as she prepared the evening meal of stew over a fire, she was stopped still. She saw slits of clouds on the horizon in a sky the color of orange like the inside of the melon her dad had brought home once as a treat. There were streaks of yellow fancying up the sky as well.

"Hmm," she called out to Bob as he tended the horses. "So this is the prairie sky."

He showed pride in her when he called back, "You're right, m'dear!"

Other times she could see in the shades of prairie grass the quilt patterns she'd worked on with her mother and Ethel after the laundry was done in the evenings. Strips of light green were interspersed with a sun-soaked yellow and then an evening deepening green.

William demanded order and regimen to keep their quest in line. "We'll be married in Cheyenne". "It will keep things proper."

She thought about proper in terms of the lack of privacy out here. With no trees or bushes to speak of, she'd watched the men relieve themselves in the open on their overnight stops. She wondered if they were bothered when she pulled up her skirt under the wagon. She had to scramble through the tall prairie grass, bending it with her feet to find a suitable place. This was a harsh reality in contrast to what she'd thought would be a pleasant trip before marriage. Many nights as they lay in bed back home, she and Ethel had imagined romantic proposals of a beautiful boy kneeling in front of them, pleading, "Won't you intertwine your life with mine?" She thought of a honeymoon as a time of tenderness and pleasure.

William went on. "You won't have a ring, but it's the legality that matters."

Reta and William married in front of a judge on a gray day in Cheyenne just before the last stretch to Thermopolis. She'd always imagined being married in a church, her mother and father, sister, brothers, and neighbors present. The courthouse at least represented some civilization out here in the wilderness.

They passed the Cheyenne Opera House announcing Lily Langtry as an upcoming show. She longed to stop for some entertainment on her wedding night, but she knew William wanted to make a beeline for their destination. She also thought things might change that night. Instead the three of them lay to sleep in their usual order in the wagon.

When they came to the edge of the Thermopolis oil field, she was struck speechless by the majesty of the mountains. The hedge stone she would come to know as Round Top stuck out of the craggy ranges circling what would soon be the town of

Thermopolis, and it shone like a beacon to her. Maybe they were home.

"Excuse me, sir. Where's the closest oil patch where we might sign on?" Bob asked of a man on a horse who'd stopped to water his ride.

"A few miles up the road, take the road to the left where it forks," the man replied.

Looking down as they wound their way, they saw lean-to shacks and only a few signs of life: a rake in one yard against a tree, a large water container on a porch, and one broken-down truck, then the lease boss appeared.

"Take your pick. Not many coming now. The oil is slow to come."

As they drew near, Reta pointed and summoned up hope. "That one. That will do us."

"Yes ma'am," Bob said, "That will be a good first home for the two of you."

She was struck by the sudden sadness that came to her; although she must have known Bob would be going on, she had come to think of the three of them as a trio.

It was only the next night after his brother's departure that William came to her on the pallet they'd spread on what she deemed the bedroom.

"I must do my duty now," he said without feeling, as though he was indicating the job of rough necking he had signed on for at this lease. He shut off the kerosene lamp, stripped his clothes, and climbed on atop her.

RETA DID HER best to make a home. On one trip when she'd gone into Thermopolis with William, he'd given her a small portion of his salary and alert for signs of trouble. She wasn't used to gunslingers and the rough crowd she encountered. But she'd bravely asked a grocer and found a dry goods store where she picked out the cheapest material for curtains to make their shack a bit homey. She'd saved back some of the money, as by now she knew that every payday William drank his fill in a saloon. She dreaded the trip home and the time after.

She understood perfectly the coldness of the other wives planted out here on the lease; the paltry work the men got wasn't life sustaining and families moved out daily. Why invest in people who would soon be gone? Still, she was surprised when her monthly stopped and the few remaining women gave her to understand that she was with child. Because of her youth, they would give her care.

Stricken at first, she was helped to deal with what the women told her was a woman's cross to bear. She had no real idea of the agony to come when they gave her their old infant clothes. She looked at them as doll clothes.

"I wish I'd thought to bring my rag dolls from home," she told William. "If it's a girl, she would have her first toy."

He simply turned away. His back implied she was at fault for the upcoming event. But she knew he had caused it.

The neighbor women had convinced William of the need for a bed for her lying in. The pain that lasted a whole night was like no other. After hours of struggle, she lay in their bed, wrapped tightly in sheets with her redheaded baby with ivory skin nestled at her breast, bound to her with a cloth. She was a woman, a mother, and the fierceness she possessed now was her strength. She'd thought her strength arose from coming here but now she saw it came from giving life. She named her daughter Roseglen. She would tame this wilderness and she hoped this man.

THE HOT SPRINGS near Thermopolis had always intrigued her, and one late autumn day when the air was light and cool, William came home to announce they were going out to swim in the biggest one. She had her mid-leg bathing suit she'd used at the city pool in Nebraska and William said he and their two kids—

Roseglen, her red-haired spitting image and Bill, their second child and his namesake—could go in their underwear.

The springs were located in a beautiful rocky area surrounded by trees, something from Nebraska she missed terribly. She tried not to think of her home back there often. It brought too much heartache. She often reminded herself that she did the leaving. The warm water gave her a deep feeling of warmth and buoyancy. She rarely felt those things, as William had turned out to be a solitary, cold man who never acknowledged her feelings, happy or downtrodden. The sulfuric air filled her lungs. Her lady friends had told her that the sulfur water could heal anything, but she hadn't anticipated that it could take away how blue she'd been feeling lately, missing family and civilization, living with an unfeeling person. The four of them bobbed around, temporarily giddy and free from their struggling life. It was one of the most glorious days they had.

WHEN WILLIAM ABANDONED her on that failed oil lease outside of Thermopolis, she was left alone with two-year-old Bill and five-year-old Roseglen. She was now the sole provider and caretaker of her children.

Life was rough before, but she thought it must be that way on the plains, especially if you're following around oil booms and busts. She'd had to borrow flour or sugar from neighbors at times, but their easy generosity made the strife seem normal. Now everything seemed dire.

The boom was still far away when he left her. There were plenty of entrepreneurs waiting around, but the liquid gold hadn't yet materialized except in the water pools. Even so, when he'd said he was going on, that he'd realized he was that kind, she knew she would stay stalwart with her children, living through the small food and water supply they had left. She would figure out how to go ahead. She was not surprised that, as on these now dry plains, dust blew through everything in her life.

At night, she played Blind Boone's music in her mind to keep away the fear. Sometimes she thought hard on the fact that she didn't miss William and wondered if that made it easier to be deserted. He'd spent many evenings at a saloon in town, stretching her time alone with two little ones far into the night. She'd thought then about Nebraska City and the joy she'd felt going to town. Although she still liked to go in for supplies, Thermopolis, with its saloons, men wearing guns, and no church or park, filled her with fear. When William came home, he was surly, ill tempered, and often unkind plus very drunk. He said he needed to drink to ease the failure of oil to appear.

She wondered if their day at the hot springs or a similar trip to Yellowstone Park had been to give her a satisfying family memory, almost an apology, prior to his leaving.

She recalled one night when the pit of loneliness had overwhelmed her full force. She had told William Ingersoll that she was having a "blue spell" and needed to take a walk. "Stay in the road" was his only warning. She didn't. The bushes had scratched her as she pushed through them to peer into the window of the neighbor's house next door. "Next door" was pretty far away, but as the gaslights rose and fell, the people inside did too.

A fiddler played, and from her crouch she could see men and women clasping each other in dance, stopping only for swigs out of a liquor bottle. She knew then that they had not been included because of her comments about the evil of drink. A few women gathered around the punch table. Because of its brown red color, Reta guessed that it too was spiked. Her upbringing made her reproachful; this was evil incarnate; women wound in the arms of men not their husbands and the trouble liquor brewed in people.

She thought of Reverend Collins back home, preaching for abstention, and she wished that for William. But another part of her wished that she could fit in with these couples. She had struck out on her own and wanted new experiences and was puzzled at why she couldn't abide what she saw in the window. Then she knew. It was the lack of control, the abandonment of propriety brought on by drink which could lead to her own possible looseness.

When the provisions for her and the children were down to their last meager lot, either providential interference or information from his brother brought Bob Ingersoll to her door. William's brother had moved on as soon as they'd reached Wyoming. Now he appeared out of nowhere late on a Sunday evening.

"You are an Ingersoll by law now," he said. "We can just take up where my brother left off."

She saw it as a plain, honest proposal. And because she'd seen a kindness in this large man that she hadn't seen in William, she was not bothered by the fact that this was her only option.

"Come on in and I'll get supper on the table," she said. The two of them took up from the left-off place.

LEATHER CURTAINS KEPT out the rain, dust, and sun on the jolting ride the three Ingersolls—Reta, Roseglen, and Bill Jr. endured from Denver to Burkburnett, Texas, the next purported boomtown where Bob planned to use the drilling equipment he had gotten through his guile.

They took a quick trip to Nebraska where she obtained a divorce from his brother. Because she used the motion of "Drunk, disorderly, and desertion," she was allowed to divorce William without his presence. Then Bob sent his new family on the stagecoach from Denver to Texas while he went on down to Burkburnett in a flatbed truck, transporting his drilling equipment. He would set up for them in this new land.

The constant pounding from the makeshift wheels and the swaying of the coach made Reta feel like she was seasick. Relief only came when she concentrated on the harmonica playing of the thin, delicate Mark Patterson, another passenger, who would play every day after lunch at a way station. It lessened the boredom of the afternoon trek. His repertoire included "Camptown Races," "Beautiful Dreamer," and "Down in the Willow Garden," and Reta cried at the sound of the notes and the vocals he interspersed randomly with his playing.

The strength she'd found at the time of her abandonment had gone away with the coming on of her illness. Songs of murder, lost love, and romance affected her deeply. She was embarrassed for the children to see her so blue from her misery. But the songs took her mind off her sickness. Being forsaken in a strange territory had left her without filters from pain. This had not come from her husband's going but from her feeling of incomparable desolation.

Leota, another female passenger, kept Reta supplied with wet cloths for her forehead from the way stations. Bill, almost three now, fidgeted constantly, leaning his head on Mark, who didn't seem to mind and who played hand games with Bill to while away the hours. Meanwhile, maybe to fill the space, Roseglen kept up a conversation with Leota, showing her mother that she'd grasped the bold, reckless aspects of their journey.

"We know, we are going to a place that's kinda lawless," she reported to Leota.

"Honey, you don't know the half of it. Burkburnett has no laws," Leota said.

Leota was returning to Burkburnett from visiting her ailing mother in Denver. When they stayed nights in the makeshift hotels that were way stations, she took the children down to the dining room so that Reta could have some peace and quiet, a thing Reta came to relish. The peace allowed some new thoughts to come into her head. Lying there, she began to have a feeling for the absent Charles Alva "Bob" Ingersoll, a sensation she'd never experienced before, and she found this mood to be the thing that made her able to endure. The feeling was hers alone, a private possession; she nursed it and helped it to grow.

He'd gone ahead to fix things for her in Texas. No one before had ever smoothed out any margins for Reta. She felt warm, thinking of him. He was a large man with a soft, kind visage, which came into her mind frequently. Truth be told, she hadn't spent much time with him at all. He'd been too busy with the preparations for leaving, and she never came to know the reason Charles Alva was called Bob, but it didn't matter. He was hers. She had a feeling this was going to be long lasting, something she hadn't thought with his brother.

Reta had a sinking feeling as the stagecoach pulled into Burkburnett. Impermanent buildings dotted the main and side streets. There were carriages, wagons, and automobiles divvying up the muddy roads that formed this frontier town. There were stories of thefts and shootings. Men carried guns. Streetwalkers roamed around, raising their silk gowns above the mud. People were living in lean-to shacks, trucks, or tents. The fields of derricks and pump jacks crowded together with fires and smoke coming up from the natural gas pipes put her in mind of what hell must be like.

She shared that vision with Bob, who had put her and the children into a hotel that first night, bringing provisions up for them.

"That's truly a visual analogy," he said.

She remembered he'd studied art back East.

With the children soundly asleep, he held her in the bed across the room, eased her mind with comforting words, and they had their first time together. The feelings she'd gingerly tended now came to life, and she knew that Bob believed in their life like she did. Afterwards, lying there, feeling agreeable, listening to the muffled voices and music in the street, she knew she was capable of weathering hell.

One night he came to the room with a present for Reta, a Hawaiian slide guitar. He'd bought it off a roughneck who wanted to move on to Colorado and needed money to travel there. After

Bob told him that his wife often sang and missed music in her life, the oil worker said, "Music is a part of me, but I'd like to sell this to someone who would use it."

Reta had a renewed feeling for Bob when he told her this and presented the stringed instrument. It was the only gift she'd ever received that was chosen just for her. She felt a twinge of sadness for the roughneck who'd put music out of his life.

They spent only a week in Burkburnett, with Bob wheeling and dealing each day, listening to the roustabouts' and drillers' stories about working the oil boom in Texas and the oilmen's stories about the business end of it. He picked their stories for pertinent information and each night after their time together, he reported his gleanings back to Reta.

Finally they came together with a plan to move on to the area in South Texas that Santa Anna had lost to Texas, near the Mexican border. Getting a drilling permit there would be more likely, and he could find cheap laborers to work his field. He'd heard that one could practically get the mineral rights in a land grant from Mexico for a song. She saw his acumen, his pride, and his know-how clearly and she began to feel good about their forming a life together.

Two

The Cornhusker
1920

Bob named his new oil drilling company The Cornhusker. Although he never told her so, Reta kept an idea in her head and heart that he bestowed that name because she was from Nebraska. Because he had found her there and—although he'd been unwilling, she thought, or not headstrong enough to tell his younger brother that he should have the right to marry this girl—eventually rescued her and won the honor to call his company that name.

For Reta, there was a line between bold and brazen. She did not want to be the latter. Her unmarried status for a short while with Bob was brazen, and it brought up images of fallen women. She did not wish to ever be associated with such. She'd not been able to marry Bob until they'd gone to Nebraska for the divorce, since she'd still been lawfully wed to his brother who had disappeared. She had promised faithfulness to one Ingersoll and had switched to the other, just like a gambler moving his piece on the table. It had worked for her, and now she was hoping that gambling would work for Bob in the oil business. Nevertheless, she would do her best to always be straitlaced, a person respected for her fine morals. She realized this could make her more critical of others. She felt conflicted because she knew that life was different out here; she'd met women who'd told her that their husbands had just switched names if things got bad or moved on and left debts and lives behind. It was the frontier—the edge of things.

"Reta," Bob had informed her, "we are like the gamblers in the saloons that you are so darned headstrong against. When we set up our rig and attempt to drill through hard rock, we're sinking money into a hole. Riches may or may not come out. When a drill works, the oil comes gushing out twice the size of the one-hundred-and-fifty-foot derrick and blows like a son of a gun; it blows bits of pipe and oil and mud and dirt. I'll be covered in oil and happy as a hog in mud."

She thought she could relish this goal now, having noticed that he was careful not to spend much of his time away from her. Never did he come home in a drunken state.

He bought a portable house in Burkburnett, because it was cheap and he knew he could get it set up quickly. One day he surprised Reta with a new Hudson automobile. After he hired a few men to move the rig and the house down south for them, promising them jobs on the oil field, they piled into the Hudson and headed to the Mirando oilfield in South Texas.

The landscape changed dramatically as they descended to the border. They began in the central part of the state; a lush region covered with bluebonnet fields and groves of live oak, crepe myrtle, and elm trees in the spring. As they grew nearer to what would be their homeland, they experienced the Llanos Mestanos, the wild horse plains, an area that was overrun with wild mustangs before oilmen and ranchers arrived. The arid land was now covered with mesquite, ocotillo, cedar, acacias, and hackberry trees, all capable of living with very little water. The soil was bone dry and thirsty.

"Mesquites have roots seventy-five feet deep," Bob pointed out.

"Heavens, if that's how far down the water is, no wonder the soil is so thirsty looking," Reta replied.

The grasslands, which the wild horses had enjoyed, were now covered only with cactus and prickly pear. In the brush, they began to see feral hogs, quail, and lots of whitetail deer. Bob told her that there were bobcats and coyotes, too.

"Why didn't they leave this to the wild horses?" Reta wondered. "This part of the world we are going to be set down in, with its thorny plants, is not very hospitable."

RETA WAS STANDING at the kitchen sink washing lunch dishes when a bellowing unlike anything she'd ever heard brought her outside. In spite of the unearthly sound, the two children napped on, so she marched out the screen door and down the front porch steps to witness the entire population of the lease— there were six families, plus Bob's office staff and the oil field workers —hurrying toward what looked like a black eruption of Old Faithful. She'd seen that geyser at Yellowstone Park when they'd taken their one trip there from Thermopolis.

She joined the running and heard people yelling, "We've hit it; we've hit the mother lode, black gold!"

Then she knew it was a gusher. Bob had drilled into a pool of oil deep in the earth, and the pressure blew it out the top. It would be years before equipment was invented to stop these blowouts. Then Bob would confess to her that even though he saved thousands of barrels of oil with the new way, he missed the excitement and the thrill a gusher gave him.

As she came closer, Reta saw the workers covered in oil, one man injured by blowing pipe being carried on a stretcher.

Finally, Reta shouted out "Landsakes!" as she recognized her husband, who was ecstatically covered in black.

Though she felt relief that he was uninjured, when he reached to hug her, she pulled away, turned her back on him—and the gusher—and retreated to her house where she collapsed on the couch, to sit alone. Fretting for over an hour, she wrung her hands and tried to sort out what she'd just seen. He had been given such ecstatic release from this gushing of oil. Why did she feel even more bound up, more lost in this barren land?

Brooding over her life since Nebraska and the repercussions of leaving her home, she reached a conclusion that she hadn't been able to acknowledge for the six months they'd been here. But she knew it now. "I hate this life! I'm scared to admit it but I really do, I hate it."

She wondered how anyone could become native to this land. The sun sucked the color and life out of the scrub brush and soil. To mitigate the dry landscape, Bob bought well-made, fashionable furnishings for her house, but nothing could keep out the dust, the scorpions, and even an occasional rattlesnake.

"I've been trying to make up a life here, but how did I arrive at this state? I am living in a portable house out on an oil lease; my only friends are the uneducated wives of Bob's workers. Bob works fourteen hours a day and now, this end is too much, too much, all of this filth! How will I ever clean his boots and pants from this greasy mess? I am strong, but can I endure this?" She looked at her bare hands and saw they were covered with a thin layer of red dust. Mother Nature was answering no.

As she heard her own words, she grasped that she could endure because she must. There was nothing else; this was the way her life had gone, all her own doing, all of it. She understood that today was the fulfillment of Bob Ingersoll's goals, his life. He was invincible. Now this brutal life must and would be hers.

She sat looking through the door into the little room holding her sleeping children. The blue curtains she had sewn filtered the bright sunlight so that lying in their beds, Roseglen on the big mattress and Bill in the pulled out trundle, her children, looked as though they were in a cool, peaceful land. She stood upright, straightened her apron, and moved into their little room where she stood looking at them for a long while.

Then she knew. She'd have to find something different for them and herself. With no local schools, she'd been teaching Roseglen herself. But today's extreme event helped her realize that she could do something more. Reta looked at herself in the round dresser mirror. She felt that her red hair and temperament made her unique: strong-willed and resourceful. Roseglen was a precocious child who remembered everything anyone said to her and put it to use in a conversation appropriately.

Watching her daughter learn had taught Reta a lot about schooling. Reta remembered having had some rough schoolmasters in Nebraska. One made her stand at the chalkboard trying to solve a math problem until she fainted. She knew teaching shouldn't be about punishment. She wanted her children to want to learn, to be encouraged to be curious.

She would help start a school.

There were other children in this oil boomtown who needed an education. Bob could concentrate on his filthy business; she would concentrate on education. It was decided. She didn't know then that her decision would start a cascade of events that would lead her daughter and her granddaughters to be teachers as well.

She sat there remembering words her mother had given her back home in Nebraska, the state that gave Bob the name for his godforsaken rig business. A cornhusker peels back the outer layers to reveal the inner good parts. Maybe couples have to do that. Her mother's words seconded that. "A couple must have each other and something else. It might be a job for one; it might be music for the other. But there must be a second thing for each of them."

There had to be layers. She was glad she had listened so well. She strummed on her guitar before she got her gumption up and went back outside. She plodded through the oil-wet mud to her husband and took him in her arms, black gold and all, on his historic day, for it was her day, too.

Three
The Menger Hotel
1929

One sign that Bob Ingersoll had become a successful oil businessman was that he engaged a suite of rooms at the Menger Hotel in San Antonio. He'd moved up in the world from wildcatter to drilling rig business owner. Wildcatters trudged around the country with their rigs. Travel, the vagabond life, was now behind him.

Bob chose the Menger because it was a mecca for oil executives. Its suites were designed for meetings and for families. The charming Victorian structure had a rotunda with historical paintings, chairs for resting, and a lovely cherry wood bar where Teddy Roosevelt had gathered his Rough Riders in the late 1890s. There were stories of ghosts, which surprisingly, did not bother his wife. Truth be told, those fantasy notions intrigued Reta. Bob relished telling the story of how barbwire had first been demonstrated outside the hotel, followed by cattle ranchers coming inside to place orders. That story meant a great deal to him because it told of the beginning of fencing for ranchers and was one of the main reasons he'd gone for oil rather than cattle. Bob did not care for conflict and he didn't want to be part of the battle over land rights.

Nevertheless, his correspondence with his brother William pointed out what a deep felt nostalgia he felt for his wandering days. Every two months or so, when he had a forwarding address for William, he secretly wrote detailed letters describing the lives of Reta, Roseglen, and his brother's namesake, as well as a little about his own livelihood.

He was very proud of Roseglen, who was growing into a graceful young woman. He even felt some responsibility for her intelligence and her keen ability to discern and handle difficult personalities. However, he fretted over their son, Bill. Bill had the wild streak his biological father had demonstrated when he left Reta. Eluding responsibility had been passed down through the genes and even though he was not, Bob considered himself Bill Junior's true father. Maybe because Bob and young Bill resembled one to the other, he felt an intense love for the boy. This often caused him to ignore Bill's flagrant misbehaviors by covering checks he signed with his uncle's name and even aiding him in finagling his way out of scuffles with the law.

January 16, 1929
My Dear Brother,

It should be wintertime, but for us it is warm in the daytime, and evening only requires a little wrap. Reta will heat up a light jacket by the oven to put around the offsprings' shoulders as she reads to them late of an evening. She reads to them each night, what we'd call high-falutin' literature, and I hope they are greatly benefiting from this. You will recall our Aunt Mim doing this for us after our mother passed. The reading is what I mean—not the coat warming. Mim worked daily to make us strong against whatever hindrances would come our way.

I can see the advantage of this for Roseglen, as our fourteen-year-old daughter now reads constantly and summarizes for us good gleanings from her books. I wish that I could say that your son does the same. Bill instead ignores his studies and warns he will stop schooling soon. I wish I had a way to show him that schooling gives an advantage. He does not have many models in this borderland from which to draw in terms of prospering in life because of learnings. He sees instead people who get ahead with no formal schooling and somehow believes that he can do the same. But I also see that he does not want to make the sacrifices you and I made in order to head out to carve a decent life. He is a very likable young man, your son, our son, but if truth be told, a bit of a lazy-bones.

I keep some of his doings hidden from his mother, as she frets over her children something awful, sitting late at night at the dining room table, reading by candlelight.

Often I find her just sitting with her thoughts. When she shares them with me, they reveal a constant worrying. She wants more than anything for the offspring to be well thought of in the world. I must confess to you that I only want for them some semblance of happiness. I can see nothing more worthy for a person in today's world. Reputation does not always give a man his peace. At least, in my doings, William, I have found it to be so.

My rig business is prospering and I hope the same is for you. Although Reta finds this land bleak and sometimes unbearable, I find a beauty in the desert. I suppose I've always looked at things differently, being something of an artist. I do still draw and paint. In this landscape there are struggles between ranchers and farmers and oilmen. I find myself on the side of coyotes, preferring open, free range.

I think of you always in thought and prayer.

Your only kin brother, Bob

Still Bob had come away from Pennsylvania with a bit of disregard for laws and rules, the parts of civilization that tied one down. He kept up small rebellions such as refusing to pay license fees on his automobiles. Instead, he used his artistic skills honed long before to create his own plates, which could not be told from the real deal. Laredo where his accountant resided was the nearest big town, and goods were available there for purchase. Bob enjoyed the banter he kept up with the Mexican police officer in Laredo, Texas, who kept at him to do the right thing regarding his license.

AT THE MENGER in San Antonio, Bob rented a two-bedroom suite complete with a spacious office fitted out in oak, a common arrangement for a South Texas oilman in the place where all the big oil dealings happened. He rented it just in time for his wife and her daughter, Roseglen, to come stay for a long weekend to buy clothes appropriate for Roseglen's high school matriculation at Westmoreland School for Girls in the same city.

On their long shopping weekend, they purchased wool dresses with cotton neck pieces at the Frost Brothers' department store, along with several sweaters and skirts, a full-swinging beautiful black coat with fur on the collar and wrists, and matching hat and muff as well as an array of silk underwear, nightclothes replete with sleeping jackets, and several pairs of shoes and matching handbags with gloves. They filled the trunk Reta and Roseglen had purchased at the same high-quality store.

Roseglen had overheard Bob say, "Let the girl get what she wants, not just what she needs." She knew that was why her usually conservative mother made no comments on the things she saw as unnecessary.

Secretly, Reta wanted Roseglen to fit in at this highly regarded school and she was glad Bob had stepped in.

Bob, too, was glad he had been successful in making the buying spree possible. He wanted to get to Reta in some way, to move her edges, to take away some of her straitlaced, rule-following uprightness. Reta worked hard on those values, still harboring shame over eloping with a man she'd only just met. But he knew that she admired his pioneering and creative side and he wanted to find a way to pass those gifts he'd been fortunate enough to acquire on to her. He loved her that much.

One night at the Menger, she'd gotten down on the floor to recover a ring that rolled under the bed, and he, in bending down to help her get up, was instead pulled down to the floor by Reta, where the two of them sat laughing aloud for a very long time between bouts of attempts at getting up, which their chuckles kept them from doing. Their merriment was unusual and almost out of control and he was grateful they could experience such moments together.

Initially, when her mother made arrangements for her to attend Westmoreland in San Antonio, Roseglen felt set up. It was an exclusive girls' boarding school, and she knew her mother's motive was to have a daughter who would be successful and well thought of in the world. But as she matured, she realized she would get a good education there. Her world would open up beyond Mirando City. She truly believed that she wouldn't care if the other girls found her unsophisticated or didn't wish to befriend her. Still, she was surprised that her mother, who had helped to start the Mirando schools, would send her away.

On her second day at the school, Naomi from New Orleans dubbed her "Red" for the color of her hair. That, plus her forthright personality sealed her entry. She stood out. She was invited to a girls-only party at a downtown restaurant, and so began a life of being "in" with the important girls that unfolded over the next four years.

She knew her mother would like this, but these girls weren't what either she or her mother had expected. She was delighted with their ways but was fairly certain her mother would not be, if she knew that they were free-spirited, intelligent, and equally eager to learn about their sexuality as their studies.

She felt a space between her and her mother for the first time, along with an independence that filled her with a delicious contentment. She fit right in with this particular group of girls who were ready to be searching and learning on their own at an early age. Her mother would undoubtedly have preferred she had chosen a different group—girls who did not stand out or make themselves obvious in any way except by being proper and wealthy.

She recognized that her mother's deep need to fit in came from her unmarried state when she first took up with Bob Ingersoll. Roseglen assumed that past was always on her mother's mind. She almost laughed aloud when in a literature class, they read Willa Cather's *Her Antonia* and Antonia was in that same unmarried state as a mother for a short period of her life.

Late nights at Westmoreland found the girls plunked down on pillows in each other's rooms, talking about the meaning of life, men, and literature, all the while smoking cigarettes. This fit her fancy precisely. She felt excitedly rebellious.

"Red," her friend Charlotte asked, "do you want to hear about my weekend? I told my mother I was going to the Menger with you, but I went with Charlie, a guy I knew back home in Tyler, Texas. We spent the weekend in a hotel in Houston. We had room service and, as he put it, 'each other.'"

Roseglen knew she was learning a great deal more than she ever could have in the small school her mother had started back home. She was learning about philosophy and art and music and began to see the beauty in math, a subject that her mother feared. She was also learning about girls who had grown up with privilege. She secretly valued having been abandoned with her mother in Wyoming and the quickening she had experienced then, along with the fear. Although she had no sound evidence to support this, she felt that she had lived through something none of these girls had and that might stand her in good stead, giving her what she needed to survive, no matter what came her way.

The years in San Antonio were divided between girls' conclaves, dances arranged with private boys' schools, and respite at the Menger Hotel. There she could go back to being a daughter or could entertain her classmates as though she were one of them. She didn't like to think about how much she enjoyed that. She knew that bringing them home to her rural life would have embarrassed her, and she would have resented that embarrassment more than the truth of her life. She knew her family would only be considered well-off in their tiny hometown.

Senior year was chock-full of dances, receptions and plans, mostly for college, some for marrying. She wasn't sure at that point what she would study or where she would go. In the end, feeling a deep sense of worry and fear as she listened to her friends' carefully crafted schemes for their futures, she decided to go home for a while.

After Westmoreland, she took a job teaching in a one-room school in Aguilares, a small railroad town close to Mirando City. She was surprised at how much she loved the exchange between teacher and students. She had watched her mother help organize the schools in Mirando City and knew this was a proper profession. Her student population was entirely Mexican, and most of the students' families were migrant workers, following the crops or shearing sheep until late October and she developed an affinity for this group. In the early forties, Aguilares was still a hub for rail shipping of peyote to the Indians in Oklahoma. One day, Roseglen saw a boxcar loaded with the round cacti, which the Aguilares stationmaster told her was for Indian religious rites. He also told her that some of her students' parents were peyoteros, gatherers of peyote, which she found intriguing.

After teaching for several years, she was informed by the school board that she had to get teacher certification. Although she missed her students, Roseglen was glad to leave Aguilares for a while and be in the college world. In October, when she took the train home for Thanksgiving from South West Texas State Teachers College in San Marcos, where she'd gone to get her teaching degree, she encountered her mother's new worry about her daughter becoming a spinster. To that end, her mother pressed her to attend the Legion Hall dance on a Saturday night. According to Reta, everyone was going,

Roseglen herself had begun to wonder if being in a girls' school for all those years had put her at a disadvantage for marriage. It did seem to be the thing her friends from Westmoreland and back home were either preparing for or already experiencing and while she still felt comfortable with her independence and knew that she wanted to pursue her degree, she understood why her mother wanted her to meet eligible men.

As a young woman, she began to recognize some yearnings inside herself. Although she had felt self-contained for the four years of high school, as she moved on to college, she recognized she had mainly concentrated on her female friendships. Now, at San Marcos, the only two males she was vaguely interested in were her history professor and a country boy named Lyndon who was known to be only interested in girls from moneyed families.

The history professor had once told her that not only did she have a photographic memory, but "with your Russian red hair and pale white skin, you are stunning." She picked out a blue paisley dress because it enhanced her red hair and blue eyes. She was ready for the dance.

Fitful, angry conversations took place each evening the week following the dance. They continued after the introduction dinner of her new admirer to her parents and those talks wore Roseglen down. She'd met the admirer at the dance and soon after, the nightly struggles began.

"He is nowhere good enough for you," her mother insisted." You come from decent people, highly upstanding people."

Meeting him had not lessened her mother's constant recriminations. In fact, the opposite had occurred. Usually, Roseglen spent these evenings stone-faced or with tears in her eye but no outright weeping.

Her mother warned Roseglen, "You will be poverty stricken; stripped of all of our propriety if you marry him, a roughneck at that!"

One night she turned on her mother angrily. "You weren't even married to Bob Ingersoll when you took up with him. You went easily with him when his brother left us in that hovel in Wyoming. How can you wave decency in her face, Mother?"

Her mother's face crumbled in on itself and her body caved too as she sunk to the davenport.

Roseglen knew then she could marry whomever she chose. For a few moments, she felt sad about the strong words she'd used as a weapon, but she needed this permission. She needed the freedom to love Robert Smith.

THE NIGHT OF the dance, she strode comfortably into the Legion Hall alone when she saw a few girls her age who were unescorted as well. Before she reached them, she was asked to dance. Oil field roughnecks spun her around the floor for several songs. She was glad Westmoreland curriculum had included dancing, but these young men fit their monikers being rough and ill fitted for dancing or dance floor conversation.

As she disengaged herself to head for the punch table, a striking man who reminded her of Clark Gable stopped her to ask for a dance. She knew she'd seen him around town, but they'd never talked. Although he too was an oil field worker, he seemed different. He looked into her eyes, held her firmly in his arms, and asked many questions. Both of them being from this small town, Roseglen understood that Robert already knew all the answers, knew she'd gone away to high school, took a job teaching at the Aguilares school, and had had to go away to college for her teaching certificate. Nevertheless, he seemed interested in learning all these things about her anew. Had she been away? Where had she gone? What was it like for her? She basked in his attentiveness.

He was over six feet tall, and being quite tall herself, Roseglen fit naturally in with Robert Smith. He held her in a protective way, his body encircling hers. Being strong-willed and independent, she was surprised at how pleasing this was to her. After the dance, he got them some spiked punch, and she began to ask him questions.

She stopped noticing how plain, with a wooden floor, this dance hall was or how different he was from the men at the San Antonio balls she'd attended. What she did notice were his coal black hair, mustache, and warmly handsome face. Dance after dance drew them closer and closer.

The Western Swing band, modeled after Bob Wills and the Texas Playboys, played romantic music in a combination of country, jazz, and Glen Miller styles. It was a perfect backdrop for Roseglen and Robert, especially when the band played—she hoped at Robert Smith's request when he'd excused himself— "San Antonio Rose." She'd always wished it were written for her, and now it really was hers. Even though it was a song of broken love, its recall of San Antonio and the Alamo, a place close to the Menger Hotel, made it seem an appropriate song for her and now Robert Smith with her. She felt certain they would not have a broken love.

Finally, they left and sat on the outside stairway of the Legion Hall. It was early fall. The air was chilly and the metal railings they sat on were cold but those details didn't bother them. Later she would think maybe it had been a moonlit night. Sitting knee to knee, eyes locked, they shared details of their lives with each other until the lights of the Legion Hall went off and it was completely shuttered.

Robert Smith was born in Texas. His father died on the farm he and Robert's mother had been struggling with down in the valley area of South Texas. His mother found a man in Arkansas whose wife had died. He needed a woman to raise his three children, and she married him.

As the baby of the family, Robert went to Arkansas with her. That man, Sam Stewart, had a hauling business there in Stuttgart, and he could easily send all of his children to college. But he told Robert that he must earn his own way, not being blood kin.

The cost of college was formidable, and not knowing what he would study there, he went back to Texas and moved through the ranks of roustabout, the rough oil rig worker position, to roughneck, the more dangerous but somewhat easier job, and finally to driller. Like her stepfather, he enjoyed taking a chance on oil. He told her that he greatly admired Bob Ingersoll, and although she did not consider him her father, Roseglen shared this appreciation. Robert was trying to win favor with Roseglen by praising the man he knew as her father, but he didn't have to exaggerate, as Bob Ingersoll was known to be a fair, honest man in his professional and personal dealings with everyone.

Roseglen let Robert Smith know where she stood. "I don't see myself only as a housewife. My years at Westmoreland taught me that. I want a man who sees me as an equal. I want to be a professional—of some sort."

As she talked, she could see his appreciation of what she said, and he let her know. "I like that in a woman. My momma was always in charge." His mother, who'd come to Texas from England when she was nine years old, accompanied only by one fourteen-year-old sister, had shown him the value of a strong woman. Having worshipped his mother and been spoiled by her, he could easily imagine spending the rest of his life with another independent female.

He gave Roseglen one chaste kiss when he walked her up the path to the Ingersoll house where the lights were still on. He saw a curtain move slightly. He'd expected the lights, and he knew that Roseglen's mother would be behind one of those curtains in the big leaded glass front window, watching their every move.

He had already prophesied that Reta Ingersoll would be a formidable opponent if he pursued this headstrong and beautiful woman. He knew that pursuing her would mean that he had to begin at this moment to be on guard, and never to be careless with his attentions to her or her family. He made the decision to proceed.

Because of her mother's adamant opposition, a proper wedding was out of the question. They married one night in front of a justice of peace in Benavides, Texas and after several miscarriages, they gave birth to two daughters, Rita, her grandmother's namesake, and Roberta, her father's namesake.

Deep within her heart lies a melody,
A song of old San Antone.
Where in dreams I live with a memory,
Beneath the stars, all alone.
Well it was there I found, beside the Alamo,
Enchantments strange as the blue up above.
For that moonlit pass, that only he would know,
Still hears her broken song of love.
Moon in all your splendor, known only to her heart,
Call back her rose, rose of San Antone.
Lips so sweet and tender, like petals falling apart,
Speak once again of her love, her own.
Broken song, empty words I know,
Still live in her heart all alone.
For that moonlit pass by the Alamo,
And rose, her rose of San Antone.

Roseglen and Bob Smith, Mirando City, 1944

Four

Dr. Ruby Lowry
1945

TWO FIGURES, A tall thin woman and a large man, their eyes met, their words crossed. Dr. Ruby Lowry had taken care of Roseglen throughout her difficult pregnancy. Now she and Bob Smith were at a crossroads. The baby was coming too soon and this kind of a delivery could take the mother's life.

"We have a decision to make, now, Bob. I know you two have lost three babies to date but think of this as a separate issue. It's about life."

Bob turned away not wanting her to see his tears. Sighing, he turned back. He knew how much his wife wanted a baby, their baby. But could she who was now overburdened with emphysema withstand childbirth? Could he stand to lose the love of his life?

Dr. Ruby had come to him out of the delivery room. Roseglen was under anesthesia, rendering her not part of the decision. Robert liked Dr. Ruby. She gave him hope.

"About life? Is this how it always is?"

"Yes, for me it is up to the husband."

"Do I have any time?"

"No, no time. This is a life and death matter. Right now, Robert."

She put her hand on his. She knew the two wanted another baby after this. She had seen them together these many months for the frequent doctor appointments. She knew his love for Roseglen. She had felt a jealousy for that feeling, a feeling that was physical when she was in a room with the two of them. It made her wonder if medicine took precedence in her life.

"Robert, let's walk."

They walked past the Virgin Mary Statue, bouquets at her feet, celebrating her motherhood. They passed two nuns hugging the wall, wrapped in black, white collars circling their faces.

"I must remind you that this is a Catholic hospital. The policy is that you have no choice. Catholics believe that children must live."

"Dr. Ruby, are you Catholic?"

"No, I am not. That is why I am giving you the choice. I can't make it but I can give it to you. Hospital administration is not human. It has no heart, no soul. When people believe they can write out rules about choosing who can live and who cannot, they are taking the role of whatever God exists. Having no luck in changing their rule, I am the one who can try to manipulate what happens.

"Well, me, after God, I suppose," she added.

He looked at her in pain. "After God?"

He felt that he was being punished. Always, every moment of their lives, he had felt undeserving of this woman, his wife. He, a lowly oil field worker, had a wife who knew how life should go.

She did not want a fancy life; she wanted a meaningful life. They read books together. She read him poetry. She did not judge people. She had always, from that night at the dance, seemed like a person who was way above it all, above everybody. But the main thing that took her up there, to the higher reaches, was that she never thought better of herself.

"May I go out and walk?" he asked.

"Yes, go walk around the plaza. Clear your head before we make a final decision. But don't take too much time. Time is . . ."

He walked quickly down the stairs, out the front door, and crossed to the plaza. It was evening and lights were coming on, birds chirping, people walking arm in arm, husbands and wives, mothers and daughters, mothers and sons, grandmothers and granddaughters or grandsons. Mostly Hispanic families.

He eased his large body down onto a bench and then realized tears were trickling down his face. He wiped them off and looked around to see if anyone had seen. Everyone was engaged in his or her own life. He wondered why he cared.

He knew he couldn't live without this woman. He could not take a baby to raise on his own. He and Roseglen had lain together at night discussing how they would raise this child. She wanted it to be exposed to books, art, and love from another human being. Although she taught him about these things, he was not capable of passing on the legacy she wanted. They were his values now but only she could make this happen.

He knew her mother and father would help but she felt that her mother's main mission in life was being an upstanding citizen and the higher things in life took a back seat. She loved her mother and understood that her shame rose from being deserted by her real father and then just taking up with his brother. It circumscribed her mother's world.

But Roseglen looked forward herself to handing this infant what she thought was important in life—as long as she could. Thank God those things were what they were or she would have married a rich oilman and not him.

He knew the depth of his desire: how much he wanted a family. When his family's farm in the Valley region of South Texas began to fail, he was scooted off to live with a brother, who became with his wife Ruth, Robert's substitute parents. He remained with them on their farm, going to school and helping out from age twelve to seventeen when his mother remarried and took him with her to her new husband in Arkansas. They had provided well for him but his boyhood wasn't what he imagined as a normal boyhood, and life with his stepfather was only a faint structure of a family. The man had his own children who took priority over Robert who vowed to bind together a family for his own offspring. Then he had met her.

As the light faded and the birds' songs grow, he thought of meeting Roseglen at that dance at the legion hall and how the feelings that flowed between them then were just as strong now. He thought of her in her beautiful blue negligee decorated with fine lace and how they lay together late in the mornings, arms still entwined from the night.

The books they read together, he sitting in his worn armchair, she on the flowered couch, leftovers from her parents, gave him a glimpse into her world of knowledge tinged with humor. They read Erskine Caldwell or sometimes Steinbeck aloud to each other. Later in the morning, he brought her coffee on a tray in bed now that she had to lie in due to the difficult pregnancy, and my God, it was hard for him to leave the warmth of their conversation and cuddling as they lay hip to hip. As he headed out to his truck and the oil field, he felt her, smelled her, and had to force himself to go.

"I might be spending my evenings in a beer joint if it weren't for Roseglen. My mother wanted the best for me but when she married my stepfather and he said he would not give me a penny to further my education, I knew I would have the life of a laborer. Roseglen showed me another way. She makes me feel dignified in knowing that the value of a person isn't just in one's profession. One's value is in what one learns and how one behaves."

He knew now what he must do.

He walked slowly back to the hospital and found Dr. Ruby now in her surgery regalia, ready to go back to his wife, to the delivery room. What would be delivered?

"I am glad you returned. I have word that she is failing so I must go in." She did not ask but looked up imploringly into his eyes.

Although he did not know nor did he want to know how his wife was sinking away, he said, "My wife must live her life. It cannot be taken away." He took Dr. Ruby's hands in his own, and looked into her eyes. "Please, please, Doctor Ruby." And then he turned and went back to the waiting room.

One other man was in the room, sleeping angled over his chair. Robert could not sit. He walked up and back, trying not to awaken the man. He was in limbo, not knowing what the night would bring. Everything could go aslant for them now. He was sound asleep when Dr. Ruby touched his arm and then shook it lightly.

"Robert, Robert, come with me. You have a beautiful baby girl, very tiny since she came so early—but she is exquisite!"

And?"

"Just come with me now!" He trembled violently, to shiver.

She didn't answer his "And?" Still he knew he must follow her, and in those minutes up the hall to what he thought would be the nursery, he reminded himself that he would love this girl, the one they had decided to name Rita Glen.

He shook more now as the doctor opened a patient's room, and he saw Roseglen's red hair spread out on the bed. In that moment he gathered strength to go to his wife's body, to be a man. But then he heard a whisper.

"Honey, come here."

Then he didn't try to keep the tears back. He flew to her and held her carefully.

"My love, my darling. You came through. You gave us our baby."

They both cried, holding on to each other, carefully, afraid this could all go away. Then he remembered and turned to Dr. Ruby.

"Thank you is not enough. Not enough at all." He went to shake her hands but she brought her little body up to hug him. She was crying too.

Then a nurse arrived with a very tiny bundle, which she placed next to Roseglen. They all four stared and stared. Rita was alive. Her mother was alive. They were a family.

Roseglen picked her up, clasped her to her breast, and then handed her to Robert. He held her in his hand, her head resting on his fingers, her 2 lb. 8 oz. weight as light as the birds he heard earlier that night in the plaza. But she would not be fragile. Rita would live up to her name. She was named Rita Glen in line with her grandmother, her namesake, and the matriarch of this family, Reta Glen Sipple Ingersoll.

Five
Reta Ingersoll's Sit-In
1945

RETA INGERSOLL FINISHED watering her lilac bushes, which she liked to do early in the morning. She scooped out chicken feed to take to the henhouse when she heard someone coming down the dirt road. She liked to feed the chickens when Bob was painting in his studio attached to the chicken house. It just felt right—him painting, her feeding. She named all of her chickens.

She talked to them just like they were her lady friends. "Here, Sally." "There you go, Missy old girl." She was astonished that she could wring their necks when the time came and laughed at them running around the chicken yard headless.

She put the bag of feed back in its place and headed out to the gate. She liked to greet guests if she was outside. She heard someone coming down the road, singing softly. She pulled off her sunbonnet, wanting to look decent for company. But when she saw who it is, she thought, "Oh, bother, it's just her. I didn't need to take it off."

Lorna sauntered down the road and began to unlock the gate herself, which Mrs. Ingersoll found a bit impertinent, so she rushed to undo it herself. "I'll get that, Lorna. Whatever would you want so early, girl?"

"How are ya, Missus?" Lorna answered, letting Mrs. Ingersoll know she wasn't in a hurry to get to her business, whatever it might be.

"Now, Lorna, I am going to head up to the colored school in just a few minutes, so you'd better get right to whatever you want to say," Mrs. Ingersoll admonished but the girl headed right on up to the porch and settled herself in the porch swing. She was kicking her feet back and forth, looking as though she planned to sit there a spell.

Mrs. Ingersoll remained standing, waiting for her reply. She included the information that she was going to the colored school because Lorna herself was colored. It might hurry the girl up knowing Mrs. Ingersoll was going to help her people. She tolerated Lorna because she admired her father, Martin, so much. When speaking of him to her neighbors, she said, "He is colored but he's a decent human being." She was surprised by his industriousness and his caring ways, but not by his daughter's lackadaisical attitude toward life.

"Oh, well, might just as well go on an' tell you then," Lorna offered reluctantly. "It's that I need a dress suit for my daddy. He's never had one, and now he needs one. Jacket and pants and all what it takes."

"Well, Martin is always so neighborly, why didn't he just come himself?" As those words popped out, Reta realized that Martin would never want to beg. "Does your daddy know that you are over here asking?"

"Well, Mrs. Ingersoll, I'm guessin' I'd have to say, no, no, he doesn't know at all. Well, really, he doesn't know anything at all, I'm guessin'."

"Lorna, what are you saying? Your father knows many things. Now, girl, maybe you better just get yourself on home and talk with him."

"Don't think he will hear me at all," Lorna answered as she slowed the porch swing going back and forth and it creaked, adding emphasis to her words. "As a matter of fact, I know it. I jus know it," and she began to cry.

"Heaven's sake, Lorna, pull yourself together. Is something wrong?"

"Well, yes, ma'am," she seemed to remember her manners. "This morning when Daddy didn't come in to breakfast, I went in to bring him awake. Breakfast is his favorite meal. He loves biscuits with that white gravy all over them."

Mrs. Ingersoll rushed her. "Stop it, now, get on with whatever it is you need to tell me."

That got the girl going. "He didn't move no matter all my yellin' and screamin'. It scared me so I ran outta the house still screamin'. Gloria next door ran right over and checked him and pronounced him stone cold dead. She told me that he'd need a suit or he couldn't be rightly buried!"

"Come on then. Come with me, quietly." Reta walked purposefully, head held high, into her house, Lorna on her tail, her head bent and her steps lagging behind.

Mrs. Ingersoll walked straight to her husband's closet, all the while hoping he wouldn't take it in his mind to come over to the house from his painting studio just at this point in the morning. She thought the world of Martin, who helped her with household repairs when she needed them done. And she knew that she was Lorna's only hope in this errand.

"I don't know why you couldn't just come out and tell me." She removed and shook out her husband's only suit. He'd been saving the suit for his own funeral, but Reta handed it over to Lorna, hanger and all. "Now, you take this straight home and get your daddy properly prepared."

Lorna grabbed the suit, ran out of the house, and galloped all the way down the dirt road.

Reta Ingersoll watched, shaking her head, tsking, hoping that the girl wouldn't drag the suit pants in the dirt. "That motherless girl was now without her daddy."

Mrs. Ingersoll grabbed her straw hat and blue handbag and readied herself to go to the colored school. She put her hair back into the bun that had come loose during the exchange with Lorna. The day before, the teacher had sent two students with a note telling Reta that they needed her help. They knew she was an educator and that she helped organize their school. She felt proud that they would call on her now.

She walked the two blocks to the little school where she saw the students playing outside. They played with sticks and a deflated ball. She entered the one-room building to find the teacher, Mary Jones, standing at the window.

Mary greeted her guest hurriedly as though she needed immediate help. "Oh, lordy, Mrs. Ingersoll, I thank you for helping us get our school started, but here it is already October in the middle and we have no books. I've called and called Mr. Williamson, but I don't even get a reply. I am at my wits' end. The children are ready to learn, but they just misbehave when I try to make up what to teach." Mary had grasped Mrs. Ingersoll's arms in her angst and, realizing that is inappropriate, a colored holding on to a white woman, she quickly withdrew her hand.

Reta scanned the room as though to ensure that there really were no books that Mary had missed. Then she turned to Mary. "We must go up to the town school right now. Gather the children. We will all go. We will let Mr. Williamson know that having no books is not acceptable. We may well end up insisting that he call Austin."

Mary had some trepidation, however. "Do you think it is okay if the colored children and I go into the town school? What if they won't let us in?"

"Mark my words—they will, they will," Reta announced, becoming brave as her idea grew. "We will simply go there and stay until we have an answer."

This had just occurred to her, and it seemed like the best way to proceed. She wished that her daughter Roseglen was not in the middle of her teaching day in the one-room school in Aguilares, as she would have liked to discuss this plan with her. Being that she had Ladies Aid the next day and then a trip to San Antonio, she knew they had to act immediately.

Mary grabbed her jacket and crocheted hat and went out to the side yard where she gathered the fifteen children who followed her in a mob, peeking around and under her arms to view Mrs. Ingersoll.

Reta addressed them. "Good morning, children. Now we are going to go up through the main street to the town school where I will let Superintendent Johnson know that you must have books. You must be very mannerly going through the streets and in the school. We will walk directly there, no lollygagging or messing around. Do you understand?"

"Yes, Mrs. Ingersoll. Yes ma'am. Yes ma'am," rang out from all of the students.

Mrs. Ingersoll placed herself at the front of the students and told Mary to bring up the rear and ensure that no mischief occurs while they took their walk.

All the local businessmen noticed their march through town. Mr. Harvey and Mr. Esterak came out of their offices, hats in hand, and nodded toward Mrs. Ingersoll. They wondered what she was up to, but she took their greetings as support and held her head high, her dark blue straw hat with a feather giving her greater status. The postmaster, Mr. Long, surely saw her on her walk, but he couldn't leave his post to see where she was going. The grocer, Mr. Paul, was the only one who walked out, right up to her, and asked what she was doing.

"Going to get these children some books," she answered.

He smiled and backed away. Two men sat on the bench outside Long's Cafe, the local beer joint, on the main street. They shook their heads in dismay. But duly noting where they perched, she was not dismayed and kept her pace, reaching the school in short order, the children walking obediently behind her.

Marching into the school office, she kept her orderly line behind her like a mother hen, and demanded to see Superintendent Johnson. She then ordered the children to sit on the floor of the office and motioned Mary into a chair. Mary sat very straight, her eyes wide. Reta wondered if it was from fear, but anyway she had to leave her to go talk with Mr. Williamson. He came out quickly when alerted by his secretary.

"Why, Mrs. Ingersoll, it is always a pleasure to have you come to our school and who do you have with you?"

"I'll tell you inside," she demanded, pushing by him and into his private office. After glancing knowingly at his secretary, he followed and shut the door behind them.

"What can I do for you, Mrs. Ingersoll?" Shuffling papers on his desk, he seemed a little distracted, and she knew he was not happy that she had arrived with her little group in tow with no warning. She had thought the shock might be effective.

"As you know, we started the colored school because we had fifteen students in town who were not being schooled. There were books promised by the state education board and they have none to date. This is two months into the school year, I believe, Mr. Williamson. So I thought perhaps you had some books they could use until the state comes through. Do you have such?"

"Why, no, not at all. We order very conservatively and have only one extra book per classroom. You are aware, Mrs. Ingersoll, that over the South many colored children have no schooling at all."

"Certainly, I am aware of that injustice and I'm glad you are as well." She is a bit taken aback. She had counted on the school having lots of spare books so now she has to revert to her next plan. "Well, perhaps, you can do something with Austin. I believe Dr. Nixon is the state superintendent, isn't he?"

"Well, yes, yes, but I am sure he is quite busy."

"He may be, but we are not. I do realize you need some time, so I will simply go out and sit with the children and their teacher, Mary, until you are able to get Austin to do something in this regard."

With that she shook the stunned man's hand, having to grab at it, as it was clear he wasn't planning on extending it. Then she retreated, silently joining her group. She heard Mr. Williamson walking around his office and then tell his secretary on the intercom, "Well, Karen, I think you'd better try to get Dr. Nixon on the phone for me."

"Hmmph," Karen replied and wheeled around disapprovingly to her desk to attempt the phone call.

When she buzzed Mr. Williamson a few minutes later, she sounded happy to report that the state superintendent was in a meeting and would not be available for over an hour.

Mr. Williamson went out to tell Mrs. Ingersoll who greeted him with, "I heard Karen. As I said, we have all of the time in the world and will remain right here, Mr. Williamson. I thank you for your concern in this important matter."

When an hour and a half or so passed, Reta heard Mr. Williamson calls Karen back in with two directions. "You'd better visit all of the classrooms and see if in fact, they have any extra books and go to Long's and get me a sandwich. I better stay right here."

On her march out of the outer office to do his bidding, Karen glared at Mary. Mary sat very still, eyes straight ahead. However, she became a little less fearful seeing that even Karen was a little intimidated by Mrs. Ingersoll.

After Mr. Williamson had the time for his Dr. Pepper and his chicken salad sandwich, he came out to let Mrs. Ingersoll know that they didn't have extra books and Austin hadn't called.

"Well, perhaps you'd better try Austin again as these children are staying here and they are getting hungry."

Mr. Williamson surveyed the children, who were sitting stone-faced, looking as though they were prepared to do whatever this woman told them to. He instructed Karen to let Austin know he had an emergency situation here, and he must talk with Dr. Nixon.

After several phone calls to Austin in which he was told they were looking into the situation, Mr. Williamson was faced with another hurdle. As the two o'clock dismissal time for the colored school arrives, parents who'd gone to the school to gather their children were upset to find the school deserted. After quizzing neighbors, they made their own march up to the town school.

When they arrived, Karen quickly notified Mr. Williamson. He told her that he had gotten through to Dr. Nixon by telling his secretary that this was an emergency. He let him know that he had a dire situation down here in South Texas.

Mrs. Ingersoll and the students heard him say that and then, "They've stayed here through lunch, and you know how colored people like to eat. They say they will stay through supper and Lord knows what else. We don't want coloreds sleeping in this school. Or fainting. You must help. Pretty soon some busybody will alert the Laredo Times and, God forbid, the San Antonio Light."

Within thirty minutes, after Dr. Nixon phoned that books were on their way, Mr. Williamson went out to inform Mrs. Ingersoll, using language that made it seem he had wanted this solution all along. "We've succeeded. Austin has shipped the books."

Well knowing the truth, Mrs. Ingersoll still politely thanked him for his hard work and a good end to this crisis. She knew she has to keep a relationship with him. She told the children to thank him, which they did resoundingly. As red faced as this made him; he stood still for it until its ended. Then he retreated, huffily, to his office. Mary released the children to their parents, who thanked Mrs. Ingersoll. Reta then asked Karen to alert Mr. Ingersoll that she needed a ride home, which Karen did quickly, probably to get rid of this bothersome woman. Bob sent one of his men to pick her up and deliver her home where she sat on the porch, thinking over the importance of this day.

The next evening, at twilight, Bob and Reta Ingersoll walked up the dirt road to the colored church and the viewing of Martin Jones' body, all laid out and properly dressed. She had told her husband that they wouldn't go to a colored funeral but briefly attending the viewing was acceptable. When they walked up to the front of the Colored Missionary Church to stand at the casket, looking at Martin, they were aware they were the only white people present. All eyes were on them. Presently, Bob grabbed Reta's hand, pulled her back, and turned with her in his grasp, his face red, eyes on the door. She looked around for a last glance at the body and then complied. She knew what was wrong but kept a serious, reverent look on her face until they made it out of the church's front door.

"Woman, what were you thinking?" Bob burst out. "My only suit? My good suit?"

"Well, mister, here's what I was thinking. Martin couldn't afford a suit and that dim-witted girl of his could not provide. So since we can well afford to get you another one, I thought it fitting to go ahead. You were busy when she came over asking, and she needed the suit right then."

"You are always willing to sacrifice those right around you for those far away, Reta. I know you do it out of goodness, but I wish sometimes there was a little more goodness for me."

Reta knew he hated fittings and buying new garments. But she couldn't admit she acted hastily at his expense, nor could she bring herself to apologize, and besides, he should be used to her never asking permission by now. It was a done deed.

"Humph," she murmured and walked on home several paces ahead of her husband.

When they reached the gate, Bob went ahead around her and held his hand on it, keeping it closed to get her attention. When he had it, her eyes on his face, he merely said, "Mrs. Ingersoll, I know what you did was right, just like getting those books. You are a hard-headed woman." His smile lightened her heart.

Years later, when all of the colored had fled Mirando City, Reta would wonder at their leaving. She had worked hard to get them a suitable education, but perhaps their treatment by most whites and the ever-growing Mexican population was too much for them. She wondered if she fought for the underdogs' rights because she was trying to appear proper or if she felt allied at times with the lowly. She felt complacent, thinking of Bob's comment to her those years ago at the gate. Although her behavior has riled him at times, she thought, "That man was actually proud of me. I want people to think highly of me; not to think of me as a woman who would just run off with any man who shows up— some William or some Bob."

That night her worries over her past did what they frequently did—flooded in on her, keeping her from being too proud. Last Sunday, she'd given a presentation at the Methodist Church about pride. She'd quoted Romans:16: "Live in harmony with one another. Do not be proud, but be willing to associate with people of low position. Do not be conceited." Tonight she wondered, "Am I too pleased with myself for associating with the lowly? I wouldn't invite the colored or Mexicans for that matter to my house for dinner. I shudder to think what the neighbors would think. But maybe with my background, I have to live by more rules than others. Is my desire for others to be proud of me going against God?"

She looked at her husband, snoring by her side. He didn't go to church and, except for a rare late night at talking with menfolk at Long's Cafe, he stayed by her side. Unlike herself, he was not a prideful man.

Six

Mary Anne
1948

ONE LATE SPRING afternoon, Reta Ingersoll, their grandmother, cleaned Rita and Roberta up after playtime. She gave them a quick sponge bath. She put them in clean shorts and shirts with socks and shoes. Then told them, "Mrs. Ellen Long is coming for a visit. You must look and act nice."

Mr. Long was a successful owner of a large drilling company in Bruni, a nearby oil town. Their grandmother whom they called Teacher envied that world, which had disappeared for her since her husband, Bob Ingersoll, had been laid low by emphysema.

Rita and Roberta attended their grandmother's kindergarten in the morning and stayed on in the afternoon until their mother returned from her own teaching job. Texas schools, unlike most of the rest of the country at that time, had no kindergartens. Their grandmother's private kindergarten fulfilled that role for those who could afford it. When the Mirando School set up a preschool to acclimatize Mexican five year olds to the public schools, Teacher decided that Anglos needed something as well. The public schooling was less to assist the Mexican children than to cleanse them from being Mexicans.

Teacher fussed around her house and kitchen, readying the living room and ice tea with vanilla iced cookies for the visit. The girls silently crept in as it was kept closed and dark except for important visitors. Teacher directed them to the overstuffed maroon chairs they were allowed to sit on. The ribbed wool upholstery scratched their legs. She told them to be quiet and still. She would do all of the talking. They knew this drill. It often happened with the preacher or other important guests.

Mrs. Long didn't come alone. She entered cautiously holding the hand of her teenage daughter. Teacher directed them both into the living room where she gave them their own seating assignments. Mrs. Long was a very attractive woman. She wore hose, a light green straight skirt, and a grey nylon blouse with pearls around her neck. Most women in Mirando didn't dress up like this for a house visit. Her daughter, Mary Ann, was pretty like her mom. She wore a light blue cotton shirtwaist dress with pearl buttons.

The Smith girls had been taught not to stare, but the girl and her mother were so angelically lovely they couldn't help stealing looks. After a while Roberta saw it. What, she didn't know. Mary Anne's face was nice except for a strange look, a look of confusion. After Roberta saw that, she thought Mary Ann didn't react the same as the other young teenage girls Roberta watched at church. Their facial expressions followed conversations, and they made agreeing noises occasionally and even small offerings into the conversations. Mary Ann didn't do that. She stared down or off into space. She didn't seem bored. She just wasn't there with them. Roberta looked at Rita to see if she had gotten this, but by her eyes, Roberta knew Rita was engaged with the adults.

"What lovely girls Roseglen and Bob have," Mrs. Long offered, looking sad at first, but then smiling at Rita and Roberta.

They giggled and squirmed but stopped and tried to look serious when Teacher admonished, "Now, girls, stop it. Say, 'thank you!'"

They did, in a chorus. "Thank you, Mrs. Long."

After Teacher served ice tea and cookies all around, Mrs. Long scooted up to the front of her chair, her back stick straight, and took the floor. "Mrs. Ingersoll, you don't know me well, but I know well your reputation. At Sunday school, in your kindergarten, and in your organizing of the public schools, everyone says you understand education and . . . well, it's been said that you could teach anyone. That is what I am hoping."

After helping to get the first school set up in Mirando City, Teacher had started her own teaching career by tutoring individual students who struggled, and then she set up her private kindergarten. She taught both very young and older students to read fluently. She was known for that skill. She was outspoken about how everyone needed to be taught some basics before they arrived at public school. Reta Ingersoll, as well as most of the Anglos in town, thought Mexican children lacked the necessary preparation for school. They thought Mexican parents probably couldn't and didn't read to their children. Still, she'd shuddered when she heard that Mrs. Harrington, the teacher in the Mexican preschool, cleansed the Mexican students of their traditional names. Rosarios became Rhondas and Rodolfos became Roberts and inexplicably Josefinas became Elizabeths.

"Well, I have done only what is necessary, Ellen. Out here, we simply need more educated people." And Teacher stared out the window at the "out here," the dusty road and the brush country across it. The rest of them followed her gaze. All except Mary Ann, who didn't change her view.

At this point, Ellen lowered her voice and her eyes watered. "Well, as you know, the town school won't even try to teach Mary Ann. I don't want to send her away."

Rita and Roberta looked at the daughter then but quickly shifted their gaze back to her mother. Mary Ann glanced up for a moment at the mention of her name.

"The superintendent wouldn't even let me hire someone to be with her to help her. So then I talked with our preacher, you know, Reverend Marshall. Since he preaches in Bruni and Mirando, he thought of you. I want you to teach Mary Ann. I don't know if you'd want her to come to your kindergarten or if you'd want her alone. She needs friends, but I don't know . . ." Her voice trailed off as she reached for the Kleenex Teacher had placed strategically close.

"Ellen, I will be quite honest with you. I'm willing to try, but I don't know what result I will get. You should know that I have no experience at this. I would like to try teaching her alone at first. Then I'll know if my kindergarten would be good for her," she pauses, "or she for the other students. Or if I can be of any help."

Ellen gurgled. Tears and sobs poured out. "Oh, Mrs. Ingersoll, there will never be any good way to repay you. We will, of course, pay you well, but this kindness will never be matched. Thank you, thank you."

During the trial period, when their mother was picking her two girls up at the day's end from Teacher's house, Ellen was depositing Mary Ann for tutoring. One day, Roberta heard Teacher tell their mother that Ellen had wanted to stay with her daughter for the lessons. "But I know from experience that never works. I asked her to go do some grocery shopping or just drive around. I know a girl that age would never learn with her mother present in the room."

"You do know, Mom. You do know," Roseglen answered.

Her mother answered, "But what I don't know is if I can teach someone who is feeble minded. Can such a girl learn?"

Again her daughter encouraged. "You can, Mother. You can."

The next week in kindergarten, Teacher announced on Friday that the coming Monday they would have a new student. "She is bigger and older than you students. However, she learns in a different manner. It is just like Roberta starting kindergarten when she was two. Only this girl is older than all of you. I want you to be kind to her. Although she is older, she will like to play the same games you play." Teacher's voice was always authoritarian but reassuring. Her tone told them she was right and that she would always protect them from anything that was wrong. Bringing Mary Ann into her school was right. The students now knew this.

Roberta took Rita's lead on Monday. Rita seemed to know that since they were Teacher's relatives, they had to be the models. Rita and Roberta usually played together. By themselves. But now Rita asked Mary Ann to join them playing in the sandbox. Roberta was jealous not to have Rita to herself. Rita knew all the best ways to play. At first, the two played in one corner of the sandbox. Roberta sat on the edge, shuffling her feet back and forth, making ridges in the sand, frowning. Seeing this, Rita invited, "Come on, Roberta, play with us." She didn't so halfheartedly. But she knew this was something they should do. She also thought Jesus would like it.

Later in life, in high school, Roberta would learn that Mexican people thought that people like Mary Ann were "with the angels" and should be treated accordingly with great respect. They were more accepting of differences than Anglos were. Anglos thought they were better than the people they called feebleminded. The feebleminded seemed to be in the same boat with the Mexicans. Someone had decided the Mexicans needed extra schooling, couldn't go to the Anglo churches, and didn't shop where Anglos did. Roberta was confused. Their family housekeeper, Florinda, was smarter than anyone she knew.

After a few days, Roberta knew that Mary Ann was a friend to her and her sister. "Reika-Robbye," she called out whenever either one of them came near, using Roberta's nickname. And then as if by telepathy, the other appears, and the three of them built with the sand or splashed in the water containers their grandfather had placed around the playground. They were just shiny new galvanized washtubs, but they were deserts and swimming pools when Teacher gave in to their begging. The oppressive heat of a Texas spring made the water play a necessity. They become a threesome. If anyone dared to tease Mary Ann for her pronunciations or how she played, Rita yelled, "I will just tell my grandmother what you are doing. Stop, Now!" and they always did.

If one of them was sick, Mary Ann inquired, "Reika-Robbye? Reika-Robbye?" until she is told why the other is missing.

Only one thing had worried Roberta that first day. It was going to the bathroom. Teacher had bathroom time right after snack every morning around ten-thirty. She had two times. One for the boys and one for the girls. They were somewhat evenly distributed, seven boys and six girls. There was a big bathroom off the schoolroom their grandfather had added on for her kindergarten. Roberta was comfortable with bathroom time.

But now here was Mary Ann, two feet taller than the rest of them. Would she go with them or have her own time in the bathroom? And then she came right in with the girls and pulled down her panties, which revealed hair between her legs. They were shocked. Then after that first peek, they all ignored it.

Soon Mary Ann learned to read Dick and Jane along with all the students. She sometimes read more pages than they did. She read stiffly but knew all of the words. She began to write letters and numbers, big just like they did. Roberta wondered since she was improving if she was becoming their equal. And if a feebleminded girl could become their equal, when poor people and Mexicans learned to read and write, would they also be their equals? Jesus said, "Be considerate of the least of these, my brethren." Weren't people supposed to give everyone that consideration? Their mother had told them of Teacher getting books for the black school that had been in their town long ago. When they grew up, they would realize that Teacher managed, at the same time, to help and to keep the people she assisted on the other side of a line drawn between them and her socially.

Sometimes Mary Ann needed to stay with them in the afternoons after the other kindergartners went home. Their grandmother explained that Mary Ann's mother often got a case of nerves from all she had to bear. She needed a rest. Rita and Roberta now loved Mary Ann, but knew the after lunch routine would be changed.

After eating lunch, Rita and Roberta napped. Teacher gently coaxed Rita and Roberta into her spare bedroom, the room which had been their Uncle Bill's, folded down the cool sheets under the ribbed, knobby-from-use chenille bedspread, faded pink with crocheted flowers adrift, offering them respite. They shedded their sandals, climbed in, and turned in unison, their hot little bodies fresh from outside play in the hot Texas sun where they created unappetizing mud pies and dug in the dirt for treasure and chase; chase always began with you can't catch me. They cupped together spoon-like, carefully not touching because of damp sticky limbs, but they lay still and close. If Roberta turned her head to Rita, she felt her moist sticky breath. Mary Ann sat in the other room, alone, straight back, stock still, mimicking waiting.

Roberta went away, drifting into a deep sleep, her hairline and creased ankles of her arms and legs growing damp with sweat. She dreamed of water, deep in a cistern, a rock thrown in to make circles, ringing down in her several storied depth of reverie. The girls were sent nightly to bed at seven when the sun still beat down hot. But this nightly time of going away was not so sudden and deep as the sultry naps. They resisted it, talking and twisting away from the depths the afternoon sleep forced on them. Then, in curved positions, they thrust down at once. Later they were woken up restless and full of unease.

Teacher woke them for their special reading time in the dining room where she kept a big rocker in front of her filigreed glass-door china cabinet. Facing the rocker were two canvas chairs. Red, orange, and yellow stripes decorated the canvas cloth. Rita and Roberta sat there. Teacher read to them, long books, beautiful tales unfolding into the quiet afternoons. Before he passed on, their grandfather sat drawing or painting at the nearby dining room table and sometimes laughed or murmured at certain passages. Roberta heard her grandmother explain to company back then that her husband was an invalid. Still, Rita thought he enjoyed the readings as much as she and Roberta. And so did Mary Ann on the afternoons she stayed. Teacher just pulled up a larger chair for her. She occasionally interrupted with noises and comments to which they paid no never mind.

One year Teacher read, *The Five Little Peppers and How They Grew*, a long sad book about a poor family.

When it became apparent that Polly was a good girl trying to help her Mamsie, as she called her mother, Rita asked, "Teacher, if they are so poverty stricken, why is Polly good? I thought poor people were bad, that they had done something wrong."

Roberta was glad that Rita voiced her concern. She wouldn't have dared.

Teacher looked surprised at the question and at her own words, "poverty stricken," coming back from so young a five year old. Teacher was quiet, rocking steadily for a while. Then in her best Sunday school teacher voice, she pronounced, "Girls, it depends entirely on the circumstances. Polly's mother is just left alone by a very bad man. On top of all that, she is quite sick. She is surrounded by unfortunate circumstances. Some people are poor simply out of laziness or sinfulness of one kind or another. But for others, poverty is not their fault." She seemed a little perplexed herself and quickly picked up the book to go on reading. Her face reddened and her eyes squinted. Later the girls would know she had been thinking about her own abandonment.

Whenever Teacher leaned up and stopped rocking, Rita would always say, "Lean back, Teacher, please, lean back." Sometimes Mary Ann mimicked her. Roberta knew they were afraid, like she was, that Teacher was going to get up and the reading would be over. Their grandmother later told them that her back would hurt her and leaning up helped. This special reading was their favorite time. Roberta didn't know it then, but they were learning about life through those books, clutching their hands with fear when something scary happened or wiggling with delight at something happy.

Some afternoons, instead, they would go with Teacher to water her yard. She had worked hard to turn this desert place into a green, cool spot. Every time they watered with her, she would weave them from tree to plant to tree, describing each, the lilacs, the mint growing under the faucet, the salt cedar trees, the umbrella trees, the orange trees, the oleanders, and the honeysuckle vine on the trellis near the back door. She moved the hoses to the round trenches dug by each tree so each got a good drink as she called it, while reciting what kind of sun or shade each plant or tree needed and how much watering. She talked to those plants and trees as well. "Here's your drink! Enjoy! Feel nourished." On days when Mary Ann joined them she muttered along the whole time, "Hmm, hmm, grow, grow," encouraging growth just like Teacher but with different words. Sometimes, under her breath, Roberta joined in Mary Anne's cheer.

It was in this oasis that one afternoon Teacher yelled at them uncharacteristically., "Get back on the porch!" Having heard a rattle, we obeyed and then stood frozen, watching her grab a hoe and chop off the head of a rattle snake in one fell swoop. Then she went right back to her watering while we stood stock still in amazement.

One afternoon when Rita and Roberta were alone with Teacher, she announced, "Let's take a walk."

They pushed through some brambles in her side yard and suddenly they were in a wilderness of sorts. Branches reached overhead so they couldn't see the house. It was dark with only spits of light coming through. It felt damp and spooky. The girls trailed behind Teacher's large body, wondering where they were going.

Suddenly she knelt down and turned her head to them. "Here it is—what I wanted you to see. I am overjoyed."

They went one on each side of her and peeked around and down to see a space-like creature's head poking out of a shell and they were frightened and held on to her shoulders.

"This is my tortoise," she said.

They looked at each other, wondering how their grandmother could own something so strange and fearsome and that they had never heard of it.

"Look on his back," and they did, only to see some reddish markings, which looked a lot like nail polish but couldn't be. "I mark him each year with a different sign. See the x?"

They couldn't; they only saw rough markings, but not wanting to disappoint, they said, "Oh, yes, yes!" and realized it was nail polish for sure.

"I give him a different mark each year. He goes away every year and returns a year later so I can recognize him." They were astounded. This was a secret they'd never known.

"Does Mother know?" Rita wondered aloud.

"Oh, I don't know—hmm, maybe, maybe not." This outer space like wrinkled creature was her yearly visitor and now it would be theirs. "We will all come to see him each year."

"How do you know it's a boy?" Rita asked.

"Oh, I just do. I know." As he started to slowly move away, Teacher said, "Let's go back in the house now."

And we did, our minds full of something new, and Roberta wondered why she hadn't shown this to Mary Ann.

Although the yard was cooler than most places on these afternoons, Rita, Mary Ann, and Roberta would still get very hot and perspire from wandering through it. Then the three would go into the dark little sitting room off the dining room to slouch in a pile on the couch placed strategically in front of the swamp cooler. They drank ice water and sighed from the exertion, the cool air enveloping them. Now Mary Ann was one of them.

She was in their lives for two or three years. Other children eventually joined in play with her as well. She became just someone to play with, like any other child. One day, she went away and they were sad. Teacher had cunningly and naturally woven Mary Ann into their play, the watering of her yard, their special story time. When they were drawn to teaching, they would know it was because of her that each child was to be a part of the whole.

Seven
Bob Ingersoll, Artist
1948

NOWADAYS HE COULDN'T walk the path from the front door, past Reta's chicken yard, to his studio. Shortness of breath kept him from it. Bob Ingersoll secretly liked that he was relegated to the dining room table in the main house. It was a long, white clapboard house fronted with what his wife referred to as the veranda where they can sat, feeling the cool of a South Texas evening finally coming on. He'd counted the steps from his table to the veranda. There were only eleven so he allows himself that.

His place at the dining room table felt regal as Reta met all of his requests for pens, paper, canvases, oil paints of a myriad of colors. He painted Gibson girls, bluebonnet fields, still-life, and ancient Mexican women proudly marching across the Texas plains with baskets of wheat balanced on their heads. The Gibson girl portraits, as he called them, were all portraits of his wife, these side-view flapper girls he gave red hair. He liked to pull the finished ones out of his portfolio, all thirty of them to stare at.

He thought how oil drilling had been his profession but now he could attend to his calling.

Each morning after Reta cleared his breakfast dishes, he pulled the easel he had rigged on wheels up to his place and began his life's work. That was what he thought of his art now. Being laid low by emphysema was surely a gift. He didn't tell Reta that, as she had often berated him for thinking an uplifting thought when he was cheated in an oil lease deal or whenever he was slighted. She thought he was easy.

Now he had the time to think of where that characteristic had come from. And as with most things, he attributed it to his Auntie Mim. Back in Titusville, his artist aunt had moved in with his mother, when his father Hamilton Dorus Ingersoll had passed on. At the time, he was a toddler, so he only knew spinster mothering. Mim was exacting in her rearing style and in her teaching the brothers artistic processes. She modeled ignoring difficulties and keeping a good face. He only appreciated the strenuousness in art and strained against it in her child rearing. His mother was one to spoil but had little time for parenting as she kept up the butcher shop and bar Dorus had managed. This produced a quandary in the child resulting in a personality that was simultaneously kindhearted and rebellious. Sitting here these many decades later, he thanks his aunt for unwittingly pushing him and his brother out of the nest. He sees her attempt at mothering after his mother's death as the direct cause of the two brothers setting off across America to earn their fortunes. He feels only a snippet of guilt over the grifting he and William had taken up to get themselves to the Wyoming territory. They would stay with families on the edge of a territory, and when their hosts' heads were filled with pipe dreams, they lifted whatever might not be missed for a while and whatever might help them set up a new life. In a manner of thinking, they were helping the left behinds to travel with them.

This morning he worked on painting the lower half of a Texas river scene and many of the colors he chose—ochre, vermilion, yellows of all sorts, brown—caused him to remember the prairie he and Reta and William had crossed heading to Wyoming those many years ago. He reckoned it was her coming to love the prairie palette of an early morning that made him turn from his original destination those years later and head back to Thermopolis to her rescue. When William had located him to tell him that he was heading down to Colorado alone, he'd asked why, not why Colorado, but why alone.

"I thought we needed a woman to care for us but when her ways turned to disapproving my habits with alcohol, I felt just like I did when I maneuvered to escape Mim's harness. I knew I wasn't that kind of man, the kind to be woman-changed. I felt more like one of them, Bill and Roseglen, her children, and I knew I was past being molded. Maybe I wasn't ever clay like."

"No, you weren't capable of being changed," Bob had replied. He remembered then how they had gone to the red light districts in Chicago and Detroit as they crossed the country. William had instructed him then in those doings. "My brother, you marry a woman to take care of your home and you go to a whore to take care of your carnal desires." He was not sure he agreed with his brother's categories of womenfolk.

Thinking of William's words about clay reminded him of mornings in Mim's glassed-in studio, sun streaming patter-like through the trees as he learned to soften the clay by pounding and kneading. He sat on the white metal stool, feeling God-like as he pushed and pulled. Then taking the loop tool to it, he could bring life to a body. He became a creator. He knew then what art was and how it could take him out of his circumstances. His mother's attempt at running the butcher shop and bar left to her by his father was a weak try at the business world. The art was the only memory that gave him a little regret for being a pioneer, for heading out West.

And remembering the same stirrings he felt when he and Reta sensed the beauty in that prairie crossing, he knew what he had to do. When his brother told him he had left her, he turned around the Model T he had acquired and headed to Thermopolis.

And yes, he was satisfied with his choice. She was his rightful wife and she supported his painting. She gave him true love. His brother gave him two offspring whom, right or wrong, he loved as his own, as though they had somehow come from him, too. He thought that somehow the three of them in collusion created Bill and Roseglen. That thought kept a thread going on in his days. To this day he felt a familial love for all of them, his brother, his wife, and their children. Even the son, Bill. The art took his mind off their wayward son. He had not seen him since all the trouble in Lockhart. He wondered at not caring that ten years that have passed since Bill went to the West Coast to escape his past in Texas. Ten years since he had seen their son.

Planning out the painting, he went over Mim's teachings in his mind. She'd slowly draw them through the development stages of a painting. First they studied perspective, making linear plans for weeks before entering the drawing stage, Then they had used the light box until he discovered he could create the still life on his own, the fruit and dishes and candles set on a linen covered table. Bill could not do so and left his brother in individual private lessons with their Aunt Mim. This was greatly to his liking, as he could not stand for his brother's sighs and remarks about art lessons being sissy play. Finally color lessons—his favorite part. The mixing to get a certain shade, a tint to match the flowers and fruit. That was what he loved these days, time to develop ten shades of blue and laying them out in rows on practice paper and then looking and looking. He developed a myriad of colors to choose from. Then he created a scene of bluebonnets. He marveled at the thought that the feeling almost matched a gusher coming in.

Nowadays Reta was the breadwinner. He knew if Bill were around him now, he would call his brother a pantywaist. He chuckled over that, knowing the power of creating to be as powerful as making money. The truth was he enjoyed watching Reta teach the little ones in her private kindergarten and it gave him time to keep an eye on the grandchildren, Rita, his wife's namesake, and Roberta. Even though the only bloodline he had to them was through his brother, he often reminded himself that it was the cord of relationship that was the tightest. His brother William cut that cord long ago.

He relished watching the girls play in the galvanized tubs he picked up at the hardware store on one of his infrequent trips up town. He'd instructed Reta in filling one with sand and one with water, thus providing a pool and a sandbox. She never made him feel less for needing her to do hard tasks nowadays. He never shared his thoughts with Reta that Rita acted like her grandmother and Roberta like himself. Rita was strong willed and could think her way through anything. Roberta would feel her way through. He knew she would have given away the rig equipment just as he did when he was set down by emphysema. He'd already been cheated out of his wells. He saw no use for keeping it to rust, while Reta saw a missed opportunity for profit. He saw a fighting chance for continuing a friendship.

One afternoon, when he knew it was coming, he calls Reta in and asked her to sit.

She sat with a puzzled look on her face.

"I've been thinking that we've had a good life, don't you think?"

Her ruffled brow made him know she worried about this new kind of talk. Although they often went over their life taken up from the left-off place, they usually didn't look at the whole. "I'd have to agree. In spite of your being laid down now, we have a good standing in the community. I often worried we wouldn't have that."

"Yes, but we also have each other."

She wrinkled her face as she bent to kiss his head and hurried back out to her kitchen.

The kiss did it. Reta's words coupled with that kiss, freed him. He fell into a hallucination of sorts. At least he reckoned that must be what this was. The wagon ride across the prairie whirred into his brain. Citrus colored suns set around him, and the hard wood of the wagon bed scratched his body, contrasting with the poking of his brother's body next to him. Then jolting riverbeds. Soon after, he heard a quiet conversation. He and Reta in the hotel bed in Burkburnett, ending with the sounds and trace of soft lovemaking. All quickly followed by oil soaked clothes and body, and, oh dear god, the unbearable joy and relief of the gusher, the black gold spouting to the heavens, the celestial place he hoped to be heading toward. And then a deep silent relief. He pushed his easel aside, laid his head on the back of his armchair and peacefully went home. In the few minutes before, he thought only of her, his Reta.

Eight

Roseglen's Unknown
1950

THE MOTHER AND daughter drove to Aguilares each morning in the early dark. The tiny town of a school and one combination filling station/grocery store was home to twenty Mexican families. On the ride, Roseglen and four-year-old Roberta talked freely, something Roseglen thought happened if people talked and moved at the same time, driving or walking. Last year, she had taken Rita, then six, to school with her and found that time with her older daughter to be worthwhile. This year, she'd put Roberta into second grade at her school to accompany Juan, the lone eight-year-old student in that row. There was a row for each grade, first through eighth.

Roseglen got this job when she was only eighteen with the promise she would finish her teaching certificate at South West Texas State Teachers College in San Marcos. She had done that and gotten her Bachelor's Degree only the previous summer. And now she was forty and dying of emphysema. She wanted to impart her beliefs to her daughters. She did not plan to impose but rather expose Roberta to these convictions, and today after school would be the beginning. But was Roberta too young? Would she remember these drives, these talks?

"Bonnie Walker is pregnant. She is going to have a baby," Roseglen told her daughter that morning. "After school today, we'll stop by her ranch for a visit. Won't that be nice?"

Roberta nodded acquiescence but only to please her mother. Bonnie's son, Jimmy, was nine years old and the only Anglo boy in the school. Often he stayed late at school because his mother was busy with ranch business. Jimmy was a ruddy round-faced blond boy—along with his cowboy shirt, this made him stand out among the Mexican boys. On those days after school, while her mother graded papers, Jimmy and Roberta were expected to play together. They never spoke a word to each other and only sat on swings or the merry-go-round in each other's vicinity. Her grandmother often reminded the family of how important and rich the Walkers were, but Roberta didn't care. She really didn't like Jimmy much, but she noticed how her mother liked Bonnie.

At school, Roseglen and Roberta sat together at the teacher's desk, the desk lamp glowing on the lesson plans and the notebook where Roberta drew. The big schoolroom was otherwise dark. Mrs. Dodier, the padrone of the school, brought them hot chocolate and warm bread for their breakfast. The chocolate was thick Mexican-style while at home, theirs was weak.

Roseglen was tall and elegant with her glowing red hair and well-made silk suit dress. "She was always a fine dresser," their daddy would say later when Roseglen wasn't there anymore. But now she bent toward Roberta, who was slight with short bobbed brunette hair. They drank and drew and wrote and ate and talked and this was an intimate, quiet, backlit time, alone for them. Roberta occasionally rubbed her mother's smooth silk hose, remembering watching her hook them onto her garter belt in the early morning as they dressed. Roberta and Rita had Saturday morning rituals with their mother, too, when they read and memorized poems, hair in pin curls of all three, and gazed in wonder at art prints. One book on Degas Roberta recalled in detail is filled with paintings of a ballerina dancing. Later in life, she would confront a dressed art sculpture of a ballerina in the Philadelphia Museum of Art. Its frozen body would sadden her. But this time with her mother was just for Roberta, as it had been for Rita the previous year.

"This afternoon when Mr. Ochoa comes, I think I'll have the first and second graders work in our grocery store and the third through eighth graders practice the dances with him in the back room," Roseglen thought out loud.

"Oh, but second graders love to dance," Roberta offered. "I know since I'm in second grade." Unknown to Roseglen, Roberta was practicing to be an educator, and she was quietly pleased that afternoon when she and Juan got to be part of the dancing.

Later that afternoon, Roberta was introduced to a new aspect of South Texas when she went with her mother to the Piedra Parada Ranch, eighteen miles down branching roads to the spread of the J.O. Walker family. She saw life on a ranch up close for the first time, although she'd been driven by hundreds of ranches and was schooled with equal numbers ranch hand kids and oil field kids. The world of cattle and horses was foreign to her because the main talk about business at her home was gas and oil wells and leases. The name of the ranch, her mother told her, translated to Standing Stone, but it sounded like a parade to her, and so she was excited as her mother turned the car in through the stone entryway with the words etched in a wooden beam overhead. She felt like she was entering a new world.

Bonnie Jean, a pretty, gracefully made up woman, was dressed in ranch clothes—blue jeans and cowboy shirt. She still managed to look fancy.

"First off, I wanta show y'all around." And they were ushered through gates and pens, walking close to horses and cattle, all of which seemed threatening with their constant pawing, swaying, neighing, or snorting. Roseglen and Roberta struggled into rubber boots from the supply by the porch, but still slopped clumsily through the muck of mud and cow pies. Bonnie took them far out through many pens to see the prize—several longhorns who had the largest enclosed area to themselves. "These are the boys, her boys, her pride." They all stood admiring.

Roberta placed one foot on the lowest rung of the fence to emulate the stance of this new vision, Bonnie, the ranch woman.

She felt that she and her mother were being schooled in ranching ways as ranch life was hurled at them.

Then Bonnie introduced them in the same way to her ranch hands. "These are my vaqueros."

Roberta wondered if she owned these Mexican men, too. Walking through the horseshit, she clung to her mother as she almost lost her footing in the filth. "You would think Jimmy's mama thinks she's walking on the sidewalks of New York! She almost prances!" she remembered her grandmother saying about fancy women. She hid behind her mother, clinging to her skirt while Bonnie spoke loudly, showing off her life.

Back at the house, Bonnie doted over her, getting her a Coke with ice and cookies, calling her, "You cute, sweet darlin'," and put her and Jimmy at a patio table outdoors.

Roberta was afraid of Jimmy, but that day he was very polite to her, asking if she wanted more Coke or cookies. She was sure it was because his and her mothers were ensconced on a patio couch nearby, swinging their crossed legs, smoking, drinking beer with chips.

"I keep all of the business for the ranch, the horse buying and trading, the siring of the bulls, the cattle sales," Bonnie told Roseglen.

Roberta sat stonily still, hoping that her not moving would cause Jimmy to find somewhere else to be, but every once in a while his mother said, "Jimmy Boy, you talk to that girl. You are the host."

He made funny, grimacing faces his mother couldn't see, but finally, out of desperation and due to his mother's constant reminders, he asked her if she wanted to go see the well. He told her he would pull up a bucket of water for her. She wasn't sure what she would do with the water, but she had never seen a well and for some reason, now really wanted to.

"Jimmy-Boy, you watch out for that little girl when you open the top. Don't let her lean over the edge. Do you hear me, boy?"

The insistence in Bonnie's words made Roberta think she was right to fear this boy; even his mother thought he could be terrifying. Roberta had seen him get into a few scuffles with Mexican boys at school, and then the muscles in his arms and face tightened in an anger she imagined could explode.

They went around back to a structure that didn't seem like a well to her. It wasn't round like in the Jack and Jill pictures but square and covered with boards and ladened with rocks. She stood stock-still while Jimmy moved the rocks carefully aside and then the boards. Finally, when the top was open, he asked if she wanted to look in. She'd heard Bonnie's warnings, but the temptation was too much.

"Climb up on this step," he pointed out. "I'll hold on to you so you won't fall. You'll see deep into the cistern. It's not really a well but a cistern."

She climbed up and had to put her stomach a little over the edge so that her dress bunched up and her feet rose up too. Jimmy held on tight to her waist. She entered an unknown world of cool darkness, and when he told her to look way down, she did. Just then, he let go one hand and threw in a stone. It fell in slow motion, and its entrance to the water spread continuous circles, opening things up so she could see into the dark water. Plunk, it broke through the surface. They giggled at first and then grew quiet. She felt she was looking into the future, a beautifully frightening dark source she'd never known about, and so as she climbed down, she asked Jimmy if he'd bring some water up for her now.

Suddenly, a shadow fell over them. Bonnie and Roseglen were standing behind them, and Bonnie let Jimmy have it for letting Roberta bend over the rim and more haranguing for letting one hand go.

"What if she'd lost her balance, you bonehead, and that sweet little girl had fallen in?"—As though it would be okay for Jimmie to let mean little girls fall in. She knuckled him on his head and he looked at Roberta, who gave him a sly smile.

Then he said, "Well, mother, do you want me to show her how we get water?" and she did. He let a bucket down on a long rope.

Roberta stood on the step again to retrieve the bucket and then drank right from the bucket, the coldest water she'd ever had. The liquid and the taste of metal almost shocked her with their strength and iciness. She turned to Jimmy. "Thank you, Jimmy-Boy, for getting me a drink."

Jimmy and the adults laughed, and she blushed and ran back around the house. She'd stepped out of herself, innocently mimicking Bonnie.

It felt frightening and very good.

Roberta was sitting at the patio table, giggling to herself, when Bonnie and Roseglen came back around and her mother said, "Come on with us into the house, now," and she followed them. They went into Bonnie's bedroom. She called it the master bedroom. Roberta had never heard that term for her parents' bedroom, but the room was large and masterful, so when the two women sat on the bed and beckoned her over, she went willingly. The room was bright pink. Roberta and her mother sat one on each side of Bonnie on the pink and blue chenille bedspread, which Roberta kneaded with her fingers.

"Roberta," her mother began. "When a woman is p.g. and she has a baby inside of her—at some point, when the baby is big enough—you can feel it move. I want you to feel it move in Bonnie's womb."

Roberta sensed that her mother wanted her to do this for some reason beyond just knowing what babies did. Although it seemed scary and odd to her, she let her mother place her hand under Bonnie's maternity top, and rested it there until a wave moved across her stomach. Roberta quickly withdrew her hand.

"There, you see, that is life; that is the new Baby Walker, living in liquid inside his mother!" her mother intoned almost pleadingly.

Roberta thought of the dark water deep in the cistern. Did they want her to see both things as dark, unknown happenings?

Then her mother asked, "Bonnie, would you let her see it move?"

Roberta had never seen a woman's belly, not even her mother's, and she wondered why Bonnie would agree to do this. But Bonnie raised her top, and all three of them stared. Again, the staring felt like looking down into the darkness. Finally, after what was becoming an uncomfortable wait, Baby Walker rolled across Bonnie's veined, extended belly for all to see.

The rolling with angles poking out seemed grotesque. Roberta looked up at the faces of the two women. They looked as though they were praying. Since her mother didn't find much to be holy, she paid close attention and tried to bring up some of those feelings inside herself.

"I had a rough birth with Jimmy," Bonnie Jean shared. "I hope it won't be that way again. I've tugged so many calves out with blood and afterbirth galore, and some of them that were in wrong, I pulled out dead. It scares me."

"That certainly would be terrifying," Roseglen offered in solace. Then she turned to Roberta. "You were born to a dark Welshman and a redheaded Nebraskan of English/Irish descent, Roberta."

Not knowing what to answer to that, Roberta quietly slipped out of the master bedroom before there was more detailed talk of birth.

When she arrived outside, Jimmy was skulking by the patio.

"What were you all doing?" he inquired.

"Oh, just talking about the baby."

"Um, mm," he muttered, so she quickly changed the subject to school.

"What do you think we will have for lunch tomorrow?" she asked.

Jimmy laughed and said, "Probably Mexican food."

"I know!" she returned. "But what kind? I think it will be enchiladas. I love Enriquetta's enchiladas."

She expected him to say something like "It will still be Mexican food," but instead he said, "Oh, I love her enchiladas, too. They are the best."

"Oh, yes," Roberta responded, and then they were quiet, thinking of the lunchroom.

The lunchroom at the Aguilares school was housed in a narrow white building holding a long table painted white with benches on each side to accommodate the twenty-four students and a chair at the end for their teacher, Roberta's mother. Enriquetta planned, shopped for, and cooked all the lunches. The lights always shined in her little lunch house when Roseglen and her daughter arrived at the school in the dark. On the rare mornings when Roseglen had to meet with a parent before school, she sent Roberta over to help Enriquetta with preparing the food for the day, which was always Mexican food but of a wide variety. Enriquetta patiently explained and demonstrated the rolling out of flour or corn tortillas, and then Roberta stood on a stool and stirred the huge vat of enchilada sauce, the tangy aroma filling her nose. Roberta wouldn't know how lucky she was to both help prepare and savor this food until many years later when she was grown up.

"Your mother is a good teacher; a good woman," Enriquetta often reported to Roberta, who wondered why she was telling her that and never knew how to respond. So she remained silent, which didn't seem to bother Enriquetta. Roberta liked that. Most grown-ups spent time trying to engage the quiet little girl in conversation, but Enriquetta understood the goodness of silence. On mornings when Roberta helped and all of the children were seated, Enriquetta came to stand by the teacher, looking regal in her white uniform and long apron, to announce the menus and that the teacher's daughter had helped prepare for the day's lunch. Roberta turned red faced, as she never knew if the announcement was from genuine pride in her or to warn the students who now teased her about how everything tasted. Roseglen made sure that after the menu was announced, the table of kids thanked Enriquetta. It was the same regard that she required at home with their housekeeper, Florinda. Roberta knew that it was important to her mother to show respect to these ladies who took care of them.

Roberta lingered at the table as long as possible, usually being the last student to leave since recess seemed wild and reckless to her, with students little and big attempting to play together. Daily at this time, her mother retreated to the school building to get some work done. There were often fights, and the big kids controlled all of the equipment—slides, swings, merry-go-round—so that Roberta didn't even try to play on them during the school recesses. She stayed near the steps and tried to be invisible. She'd gone to kindergarten at her grandmother's private school, and there Teacher controlled all of the activities, so boys couldn't fight or threaten the little ones. Sometimes if an older boy teased Roberta about being the teacher's pet, the fifth-grade girls threatened to tell her mother. Roberta knew she was in an odd place between student and teacher's daughter, and so she was comforted when her mother rang the hand bell to come in.

Back at school, she thought that perhaps now Jimmy was her friend. She noticed that if any of the other pupils teased her, Jimmy moved in and stood by her and things changed in her favor. Still, the two of them didn't talk but they often exchanged knowing looks, which helped her to be more comfortable at school in her mother's work world.

A few days after the trip to the ranch, Roberta knew why it was important for her to feel life in Bonnie Walker's tummy. On a Sunday afternoon, her mother came out to the front porch where

Rita and Roberta were playing jacks to say, "We need to have a conversation, girls."

She sat on the picnic bench seat, one girl on either side, and pulled Roberta to her, holding her close in her arms. Rita, maybe because she was older, sat upright, her eyes never leaving her mother's face, while Roberta looked out over the white caliche hill they live on.

"Girls, you know that I have emphysema and have gone to clinics and doctors all over. They can't help me now. I'm going to have to go away. We have talked a little about death, and I have read you many poems about it. I want you to be prepared, to know. I will probably be dying in a few months. I will always love you. Your father and grandmother will take care of you."

Afterward, as Roberta sat alone on the porch, she dragged her sandals over the white cement floor pocked with bumps and little black stones and knew that she wanted to remember everything about her mother. Her mother bequeathed to her swollen bellies with elbows poking out, ripples in cool dark bodies of water, respect for all people, calves being pulled out of their mothers, all that along with art and poetry, the stuff of life and death. Roberta looked down into the wide unknown.

Nine

Anne Frank and Roseglen
1951

AT FOUR P.M., she left her school in Aguilares, turned at Three Points Beer Joint to head home. She was tired. Her throat ached from the long day, talking and coughing. She scanned the parking lot for his truck. She didn't mind if Robert stopped for a beer occasionally but she asked him to pick up the girls from school tonight. His beat-up dark green Chevy pickup wasn't there. She was glad. She'd be happy to reach home.

On the final mile she thought over her day. She enjoyed hearing Rogelio and Juan Martin, her two eighth grade boys read their essays on travel. Travel meant something different to Mexican students in this all-Mexican community.

Juan wrote about traveling to Colorado to follow the crops. Rogelio wrote about fleeing the Border Patrol with his father coming across the Laredo-Nuevo Laredo border. When she read them the assignment out of their geography books, she'd opened up the lesson, telling them it could be a trip taking an uncle to the hospital, a trip to Colorado to shear sheep, a trip driving the girls' basketball team to Agua Dulce, or a trip to meet relatives hiding under mesquite trees having crossed into Texas. She watched their faces, the faces of all the students.

Juan slowly, respectfully raised his hand. "Miss, I thought the book was talking about a trip, going to Nuevo York or to Mexico City."

She answered, "What do you think I am talking about, Juan?"

"I think you are talking about us, about our travels."

The room was pin quiet. Every student from first to eight grade focused on her face.

She smiled a sneaky, little smile. "You are correct. Sometimes the book has to be reinterpreted or changed to fit the circumstances, to fit the students."

"Okay, ma'am," he responded politely. "We got it. You got it."

All afternoon as they wrote and wrote, She felt a satisfaction. When they read their writing to the whole school all eyes were on them. Some mouths agape.

Arriving home, she found Rita and Roberta doing their homework in front of the Philco radio/phonograph, listening to swing music on one of her records. She kissed their heads and headed to the kitchen to see what Florinda had left for supper. Robert had already set the table. He took her in his arms, and they danced around the kitchen until her breathing was heavy. He kissed her cheek and sat her down in a chair.

"Come on girls, let's eat. I know your mom wants to keep reading tonight."

She smiled. She remembered how last night as she began to read *The Diary of Anne Frank* to the girls, he had pretended to read his James Thurber book but she could tell he was listening the whole time. She acted like she didn't notice; she wanted him to listen, thinking she didn't know.

They ate quickly. Everyone wanted to get back to the story.

Robert cleaned up the kitchen while the girls and Roseglen changed into nightgowns, combed their hair, and brushed their teeth. Then she settled into the green flowered couch, a daughter on each side. She looked at them both, tousling their hair; she wanted to remember the feel of their bodies leaning into her. Bob settled into his worn corduroy armchair and picked up Thurber. They were both in their usual reading places.

Some nights after the girls are asleep, they read aloud just to each other.

She began.

Anne was talking about what bothered her the most: "Not being able to go outside upsets me more than I can say and I'm terrified our hiding place will be discovered. And we will all be shot."

Rita asked, "Why can't they go outside?"

Both Roseglen and Bob were silent for a few minutes. They exchanged looks. She thought about why she was reading this to her girls. She knew perfectly well that they were too young, much too young. But it was something she must do. She spent a lot of time thinking about what prejudice was and where it came from. She thought it was an attempt to cure an inferiority complex. The more she learnt about that evil little man in Germany, the more she knew he felt so deeply inferior that he had to make himself superior over others. He lorded it over the Jews. He used work, guns, fires, destruction, and in the worst scenario, ovens to make himself puffed up over a people whose flesh, skin, word formation, and shape of eyes, noses, and bodies and lips were different from his. He wanted to erase difference. She needed a six year old and an eight year old to understand this. That an evil man killed people because of their religion, their food, their rituals, their bodies was not a lesson she could leave this earth without teaching her children—the injustice of this deeply evil page in the history of the world.

They were all staring at her, waiting, knowing she was deep in thought. She did a lot of this now and they tolerated it well. "Remember the Frank family is in hiding with their friends, in an attic."

"And," Rita offered, "they cannot go outside ever. They can't even look outside except to peek in the middle of the night. They have to be quiet all day long whenever the office is open downstairs. They can't walk around or talk."

"Like our nap time."

She read. "We're still as baby mice. Who would have guessed three months ago that quicksilver Anne would have to sit so quietly for hours on end and what's more that she could?

Countless friends and acquaintances have been taken off to a dreadful fate. Night after night, green and gray military vehicles cruise the streets.

"They knock on every door, asking whether any Jews live there. If so, the whole family is immediately taken away. If not, they proceed to the next house. It's impossible to escape their clutches unless you go into hiding . . . No one is spared. The sick, the elderly, children, babies and pregnant women—all are marched to their death.

"November 1942."

The night before, Roberta had asked where the people were taken. She'd told them to camps, death camps, where they would be killed. Her stomach ached from saying those words to her girls. What did they know of death? Their father had taught them to use a rifle by shooting at cans. He knew she didn't care for guns but he owned rifles for hunting and protection out on the lease. They knew Bob Ingersoll died. They saw him head down on the dining room table the afternoon he passed away at home. But he often napped liked that. When their grandmother sent them out to wait for her by the gate that day, they had never known death. Once she had them in the car with her, she told them that he had died. "And we will all die."

"Like Jesus," Rita offered.

"Yes," she said, "like Jesus."

"And he arose," Rita added proudly.

Roseglen didn't respond. She was thinking how her mother's teachings had won out over hers.

She continued to read:

"We long for Saturdays because that means books. Ordinary people don't know how much books can mean to someone who's cooped up. Our only diversions are reading, studying and listening to the wireless.

"July 11, 1943.

"What does this remind you of, girls?"

Roberta eagerly offered, "Going to the library up those stairs in Laredo, Mother. Getting books for you."

"And books for you as well. Always remember that books take you everywhere, teach you lessons about how to live," she offered.

Then they were all quiet again. She was wondering if they were thinking she could escape death through reading. In a way she did, but didn't think she could explain that to them. Why was death always there now, beating down the door? And was she inviting it closer by reading this book to them?

She returned to the book:

"The nicest part is being able to write down all her thoughts and feelings; otherwise I'd completely suffocate."

Rita asked, "Mother, what is suffocating?"

She told her that it was similar to when she couldn't breathe. "If a person can't breathe at all, they die."

Everyone was solemn and quiet. She knew they were worrying about her suffocating now. She was trying hard to face this. That it would be harder for all of them, Bob and Rita and Roberta and her mother, if she was fighting against it day in and day out. Last Saturday as she sat with Dr. Malakoff, she asked, "Is there any way, any way at all?"

He took off his glasses and turned fully toward her. She saw his eyes were wet. "No, Rose, none at all. You know I would do all I can. The report from the clinic in San Antonio is definitive. We can do nothing, nothing at all."

She looked at him then searchingly, hoping he had a way to guide her through this ending. She could tell he knew what she wanted but he turned back to his desk and wrote out her weekly prescription.

"I will see you next Saturday." He'd stood and hugged her.

She was thinking that maybe she was reading this not so much for her girls as for herself.

"Honey, I think it is bedtime." Bob brought her out of her reverie. She knew the reading ended like this each night but she saw strength in her girls tolerating this. Their searching of her face and her words and Anne's words, not for a way out of it but a way to endure and more importantly, a way to be in the world. What to fight against; what to be intolerant about.

Ten

Saving Booker T
1951

RITA AND ROBERTA waved their hands through the cloth, batting the sheets and towels, floating through the sweet-smelling material blowing on the clothesline in the side yard. Florinda hung up linens from the laundry basket farther up the line. They buried their faces in the sheets, the clean smell filling them up, soap and sun.

"Please, please, Florinda. Take us for a walk. We want to take a walk. Can't we go up the other hill?" Rita and Roberta were a chorus.

She was a beautiful woman with a strong brown face. Their Daddy jokingly fought with her. She loved to rearrange the furniture when she cleaned. Every week he asked her to please not move his armchair, the place he rested and read in after dinner. She always moved it and smiled at his frequent requests to stop this. He said she was stubborn. "More like an Indian than the other Mexicans." They knew he knew what she did for their family. To the girls, she was a part of their family. She was always been there. Nowadays, they wished she didn't have to go home at night so she could care for their mother in her illness. They knew she went home for Mariana, her girl, but Mariana was a teenager and they thought teenagers could care for themselves.

Their father was somewhat right when he called Florinda an Indian. She was almost certainly a Mestizo as most South Texas Mexicans were. They were from a three-tiered heritage—Mexico, Spain, and Azteca, a blending of cultures.

Roberta's family was living in their second home on a hill their parents had bought in Mirando City. They liked this house the best but still loved to go exploring the other hills nearby.

"I have to work, girls. Many, many things to do for your mother."

"Yes, yes, please, please, just for a little while," Roberta begged, looking around a sheet into Florinda's dark brown eyes.

"You know Mother won't let us go alone. We must! We must! We will be good. It will be okay. We won't get hurt," Rita promised.

"Oh, you girls can get me in such trouble."

"Yeah, yeah!" They squealed. They knew she had given in.

"Go get on shoes, now. We may run into thorns."

The girls galloped into the house, searched their bedroom floor for matching shoes, and flung themselves out the door, nearly knocking Florinda and her wash basket over. They were quickly ready and waiting.

The early morning was cool and still. "Let's go walk around the oil tanks. I know you girls are never allowed there alone, so you hold my hands. I like it, the tanks."

They ran and screeched around Florinda as they headed off their hill, occasionally grasping her hands and then running free. They knew she loved these walks as much as they did. Sometimes she told them about her life or her plans for her daughter, Mariana.

They bounced down the caliche-covered pathway, a small Mexican woman in a long flowered skirt and sweater, trying to hold the hands of two little jumping girls, excited to be on an adventure. The girls both had short boy-cut hairdos. Their mother had begged her hairdresser to give them the cuts. Their grandmother had been angry. "Oh, Roseglen, why do you want them to look like boys? Don't you want pretty little girls?" Roberta loved the haircut. It felt good in the cool morning air. She liked to string her fingers through the short strands.

"Oh, no, aye yi yi." Florinda suddenly startled. "Your dog, your dog. He follows."

"Yes, yes," Rita yelled. "Booker T loves walks."

Their black cocker spaniel joined them, sniffing the ground, bounding and circling around them. Roberta captured him for a hug. She loved this animal. It would be several years before the girls would wonder why their parents had named him Booker T. Then it seemed disrespectful. They hadn't thought their parents were prejudiced like many of the folks in Mirando. They would puzzle over this together years later.

"Look, girls, he wants to protect you. Like I protect you. Did I tell you when I am a little girl in Mexico, I have a dog? It was not like your dog—mine big, lazy, perezoso."

"Oh, what color was he? What did he like to eat?" Roberta squealed. She already knew he was black and white spotted, and that he liked to eat pinto beans. But she loved to hear it over and over.

"And that was not fun for nose!" Florinda reported. "All day he slept, all day. Eat, sleep, eat, sleep. Now I have no dog. That is good. When Mariana goes to college, she won't be sad to leave dog." Rita had heard her parents discussing Florinda's plan to send her daughter to college. They fretted over how she would afford that on a housekeeper's salary.

When they reached the top of the next hill, Florinda abruptly stopped her story. "Look, look, girls. The men fill the overflow pool with oil. We must not be here. Go back." She flapped her hands toward the girls' backs, trying to wave them away.

"Oh, let us go up and see the oil, please, please." Both girls pulled on Florinda's arms, begging. "Just for a minute. That is all!" The girls loved that Florinda was always unsure who was in charge and so usually did their bidding.

AT ANOTHER LATER time, Roberta would go to another overflow oil tank in forbidding circumstances. Mr. Venecia, her high school science teacher, got word that an overflow tank north of town had caught fire. He said to his little senior class of seven that since it was a once-in-a-lifetime opportunity, they would go.

"How?" JoBeth asked. "Pile in my car. You can stay back if you wish."

They all rushed out the front door with their teacher, only to be hailed by the superintendent, Mr. Long, "I know what you're doing, David." Faculty never used first names in front of the students.

Mr. Venecia spoke back with the same excitement with which he taught algebra. "I know you do and I know what I'm doing. It has to happen, Mr. Long. Let's go, kids!" It felt dangerous even before reaching the fire, this exiting against Mr. Long's will. And we went.

It would be the only time Roberta would see such a fire. Tongues of flames rose to the sky like a fury, red flames in dark clouds of smoke and fumes. The air was stifling. They piled out of the car but stayed near when Mr. Venecia warned there could be explosions and they'd need to escape. Roberta had butterflies in her stomach. She wanted to be there. She knew Mr. Long and her grandmother would not want her there. She felt adventurous and scared, knowing she was breaking a rule. She realized Mr. Venecia had those same trepidations.

Perhaps thinking his job might be on the line, he said in what felt like a very few minutes, "Let's go now. We've witnessed this. Get in the car."

Roberta knew he was thinking of his wife, whose anger would be like this fire if he lost his job, disobeying. They slunk into the car, four piled in the backseat, three in the front, talking of the leaping flames all the way to school, where they silently walked back to class, clasping their secret close.

Always needing to confess, that night Roberta told her father. "Daddy, today we saw something unbelievable. I know you've seen it. Mr. Venecia took us to the fire. Mr. Long didn't want him to, but he said we should see it."

In a conspiratorial voice, her father replied, "Well, I'll be. I'll be damned! It's probably the only time in your life you'll see that. I've only seen it two times. I went out there, but I never in the world thought you'd go. Well, I'll be damned!"

Roberta realizes he was proud. And that Mr. Venecia, that man who'd shown up to teach them in his little green Buick, fresh from Texas A and I College in Kingsville, would show them a different world from the one they were used to.

THEY STARTED UP the rim and saw the overflow next to the big white oil tank, now full of the black gold. They had all forgotten that Booker T was along. They turned as he began leaping and barking and jumping. They all rushed toward him, but the liquid had excited him, and he jumped right in.

"Oh, *dio*. Oh, dio. Your puppy, your dog! I told you we shouldn't come. He can die."

Both girls started crying, yelling, screaming, "No, no, save him. Save him, Florinda. Now, save him."

They knew she could. They knew her strength. They knew she kept their family together in the rough times now. With their mother unable to breathe or often to get out of bed, Florinda did everything. She cleaned, took care of the girls, washed the clothes, and cooked all of the meals, leaving the supper ready when she departed at five. That was how much she loved them. They believed her love protected them.

Shrieking "Booker T, Booker T, come back!" they wound their arms around each other to keep each other from falling in.

"Get back! Get back now!" Florinda yelled at the girls, something she never did; she was a quiet woman. Their father said she was so silent because she was keeping secrets. He said it was the secrets of her tribe.

They were sure their dog would die.

"It will be like Mrs. Evans," Rita said. "Did you see her yesterday, Roberta? Mrs. Evans? She was already a ghost, so white. He will finish also! Booker T will die. Just like she did last night!"

"No, no, no." Roberta heart was breaking. "Don't let him, Florinda!"

YESTERDAY, THEIR GRANDMOTHER was called upon to "sit up" with Mrs. Evans. Whenever someone was dying, the older women in Mirando create a "sitting up" schedule to take turns stationed by a bed, holding a glass of water to parched lips, wiping a forehead with a cool cloth, keeping the curtains shut and keeping the light away. They helped the dying person to cross over, to have a smooth parting. "No one should ever die alone," their grandmother said. The thought was comforting.

Reta Ingersoll had called their home from her time with Mrs. Evans, which was early evening until midnight, to ask their dad to bring the girls to her. "Bob, they need to see Mrs. Evans, to say goodbye. She has been a shut-in for a long time. It's coming soon." He knew that his mother-in-law thought this would help the girls to deal with their mother's upcoming departure, so he agreed.

The girls were shocked. They had only seen Mrs. Evans occasionally. She was not a church-going lady, and she didn't attend their grandmother's canasta parties when they lurked around, listening to gossip. Nevertheless, they got into dresses and put barrettes into their hair. They were ready. They knew they had to go. They knew that they were called on now to do things they didn't understand. Roberta looked inquiringly at Rita. Sometimes she knew the whys. Roberta could tell that she didn't know this time. Rita's little round face was fixed in a worrisome frown that frightened Roberta.

They crawled out of the car, listening to their daddy tell them he would retrieve them in thirty minutes. It sounded like an eternity.

Mrs. Evans lived in an enormous wooden white house with tall windows on both floors. It was porchless, which made the walk up to the door feel strange. The house was tired, sagging. They lollygagged on the steps. They'd never been here before. Rita knocked softly and then louder when no one answered. Finally, their grandmother pulled them in, whispering.

She looked tired, her eyes red. "Now girls, I know you don't know Mrs. Evans well."

Rita thought, Not at all.

Their grandmother continued, "She won't make it through tonight. She'll probably die on my watch, which is until midnight. I want you girls to see how calm she is. I want you to see for yourselves that death can be peaceful."

As their eyes adjusted from the bright sunlight outside, they saw a high bed, angled at the side of the living room. Everything else in the room was dark. Thick curtains covered the tall windows. The bed and the figure shone bright white. Their grandmother guided them gently toward Mrs. Evans. There was one chair for the sitter, and Reta Ingersoll sat her large body down on it and placed the girls on either side of her. They held on to the arm of her chair and stared. They'd been taught that staring was impolite, but they knew now was a time for looking.

Mrs. Evans was laid out flat, her body covered by a white flannel blanket drawn up over her shoulders. The girls could see her white nightgown collar ruffled around her wrinkled, skinny neck, which was sticking out like a chicken's. Her face was as pale as the nightgown and the nightcap warming her head. Her eyes were closed, her bluish lips pursed tightly. Rita wondered if nightcaps were required in death or somehow assisted it. Veins shone out of Mrs. Evan's pasty white face.

Was this what one looked like in death? Roberta thought. She wonders how her mother would look. Would she wear all white with a nightcap?

"Go ahead, girls, say something to her," their grandmother admonished.

Roberta looked at Rita in astonishment when Rita began aloud, "Now I lay me down to sleep. I pray the Lord my soul to keep," their nightly prayer. Roberta joined in. "If I should die before I wake, I pray the Lord my soul to take."

"Teacher, is death like sleeping?" Rita asked.

Both girls looked up into their grandmother's eyes, which were moist now. "Why, yes, how clever of you, Rita. Death is perhaps a long, long sleep. A sleep in heaven."

Roberta wondered how Rita had been so smart as to speak their prayer about sleep at the right time. It was now clear to her that Mrs. Evans had laid down to sleep—to die. At first, coming into this darkened house, being forced to view someone dying, had made her feel frightened. Now the idea of sleep softened her worries of dying and, in particular, her mother's death.

"Can she wake up from the long sleep, Teacher?" she inquired.

Teacher now took each of the girls' hand. Her hands were cold. Her bent arthritic fingers grasped theirs lightly. "Oh no, dear. No, no. Death is final, complete—an ending, God rest her very soul." Her body suddenly shuddered. She told the girls she must go freshen Mrs. Evan's water. She stood up, released their hands, took the tray with the glass and pitcher, and left them alone at the deathbed.

NOW FLORINDA DOVE into the brush by the overflow tank. The two clinging girls had a bead on her every move. She wrestled a large branch from a mesquite tree. "These skinny trees, no good, "she yelled. "Too little. But I try, I try. This the biggest," she said of the long, fat branch tightly clasped in her hands.

The girls felt hotter as the sun is rising. They squatted down to peer into the tank. The dog was mucked into the oil, trying to move, trying to swim. He struggled and wiggled. Roberta thought that if she fell in, she would be boiled. The sun beating on the oil made it seem to be cooking.

Florinda poked the branch toward him, hoping he would manage to climb aboard. The stick looked as though it was stirring black molasses. He couldn't climb up. He was a glob, a large blob of muck, no longer a dog's body. Realizing that he wouldn't be able to help in his rescue, Florinda used the branch like a shovel. Then unable to scoop him up, she pushed and prodded the goop that was the dog toward the edge of the tank, which now had become a shore, a shore for Booker T to reach.

She yelled, "Rita, run to the house, grab a towel from clothesline. Quick. Go fast!"

Rita ran faster than she ever had and brought a towel back in what seemed like no time to Roberta. Roberta's heart was beating fast; she'd never been so terrified. She loved this black cocker spaniel. She spent hours talking with him and her cats. She was often afraid to talk with people, but he was her friend. She could use her voice with him.

Florinda had pushed Booker T to the edge of the oil rim. Her short taut body leaned over to bundle him up in the towel. Now she, too, was screaming. Holding the moving mess frightened her. She tried to hold him apart from her body while keeping him in her grasp. As she walked and ran with him, she wept and kept bundling to stop him from writhing out of her arms.

The girls couldn't keep up, but they stumbled down the oil tank hill and then pushed up their hill to see Florinda dumping Booker T into the washtub left over from her morning wash. She instructed Rita to bring her the hose and turn the water on at the spigot. Florinda wiped the dog's eyes and mouth and ears while waiting for the water. Rita accomplished her task in moments. Then on further instructions, she and Roberta pulled towels off the line. They couldn't reach the wooden clothespins so they yanked and pulled, bringing all of the towels on the line to the ground, and then rushed them to Florinda.

She put her thumb over the mouth of the hose to spray the dog's sodden body. With his openings clear, Booker T was now relaxing from the stress; he rested in the tub. Florinda retrieved some laundry detergent and began to suds him. Suddenly, bubbles pour out of the tub, and Booker T finally yipped and barked and licked Florinda's hands in obvious gratefulness.

"Oh, you bad, bad dog, you wild like coyote," she scolded, but her voice was warm, caring. She washed and scrubbed and dried, and washed and scrubbed and dried, emptying the tub for fresh rinses many times. The pile of towels rose. Rita and Roberta circled around the scene, full of relief and excited now by the bubbles. They had been certain their dog would die.

Then a new worry arises. "Oh, Florinda, we can't let him be out here. He will go back. Oh, what can we do?" Roberta asked. "He is not a house dog. No, No." She began to cry.

"He will go back, Florinda," Rita said. "We must take him into the house."

"Girls," Florida said, "he is not stupid dog. He won't want this. He is smart dog."

They regained their confidence in their caretaker and Florinda let them do the final drying off. The dog was so tired he sat very still for their rough-and-tumble drying. They felt good participating in helping Booker T. Still sopping and bedraggled, he slunk off to the side porch to rest.

Florinda invited the girls for a morning snack. "We deserve it, girls."

They went into the kitchen where Florida prepared warm tortillas with cheese and chocolate milk.

Rita sang praises. "Florinda, you did it. You saved Booker T. You did it by yourself. We were screaming and scared. You saved our dog!"

Roberta sat, chewing quietly, pondering what to do. She wanted to thank Florinda, but she was shy. She didn't know if she should compliment an adult like Rita had. She was only a child.

She talked with cats and dogs for companionship. Florinda had caught her doing it recently and teased her. "What's wrong with you? You talk with animals. Being crazy, Roberta!" What would her words be to a grown-up, and particularly to Florinda?

She sat on the steps of the porch where she usually chatted with the family of cats or Booker T and thought over the events. She was still shaking; her heart was beating only a little slower. Florinda proved herself. She was a savior. Maybe everything would be okay. Florinda had told her that she lit candles in the Catholic church for Roberta's mother. She had said that God could make her well, that God could do miracles. Maybe her mother didn't have to go into that long sleep after all. Today's events showed Florinda's strength. Maybe Florinda could reverse the downhill path the family was taking; maybe she could make them whole again.

Eleven
Underwater
1952

AT AROUND FOUR o'clock on a Sunday afternoon, Bob Smith, who refused to plan ahead, announced excitedly, "Okay, gang, let's pack up and go to Leakey right now!"

The whole family rushed around. They packed suitcases. The adults made phone calls, arranging details for the girls' grandmother to feed their dog and cats, to keep an eye out on their house. They piled into the car around eight o'clock in the night and took off from South Texas to the Hill Country two hundred miles away. They were going to their favorite cabin by the Frio River near, Texas.

They usually started out in early morning and drove all day. This was the first time the two girls had been on an all-night car trip. Rita and Roberta fell asleep on pillows in the big soft backseat after eating baloney sandwiches, washed down with milk in little glass bottles. They woke every once in a while to watch the stars or the occasional light on a pole brightening up a little ranch with a windmill, a barn, or a tiny house. These things flashed by, intermingling with their dreams. They watched the two heads in the front seat, moving, talking, the coal black hair of their father and their mother's glistening red hair.

At one point, they heard their mother say, "Bob, you are drifting off. Pull over, please."

Their dad, ever accommodating, pulled off. They all slept by the side of the road for what their mother considered an adequate period of time. Then their Daddy took off again. They were exhilarated and a little scared of this nighttime adventure.

They arrived in Leakey around four in the morning, and by the time they got out to the cabin and put everything inside and got beds made, light was coming on outside.

"Right now I'm not going to bed. I'm going fishing. Early morning on the river is the best," Daddy declared.

Rita and Roberta rolled their eyes at each other because they'd heard him say that it was evening when the fish are jumpin'.

"Who wants to go along?" their daddy asked.

Although she was about to put on her pj's, Roberta immediately volunteered. She always liked to do boy things. She knew her sister wouldn't consider it.

Her Daddy did, too, as he said, "Come on, Rob, get on a long-sleeve shirt and we'll head on out to see if we can catch us some fish."

Roseglen walked them to the door and said, "Be good, you two."

She kissed them both, Roberta on the top of her head, Daddy on his cheek.

It felt special to Roberta to have time just with him. Up until today, she'd only gone fishing in ponds and tanks near their hometown. Now she was finally going to go fishing in the river. They got in the car and drove back into Leakey, a tiny tourist town with log cabin motels and funky cafés. She asked why they weren't going down the river road. Her daddy said that no one could ever fished in the early morning without coffee.

They stopped at their favorite café where the waitress, Ellen, whom they knew from other summers, said, "Hon, how special is it for you to be out goin' fishing with your daddy at this time of the morning?" She made them two big cups of coffee to-go with milk and sugar. This was Roberta's first coffee, so she was feeling doubly special.

They headed back and turned down the river road, parked on the side, and got the gear out of the trunk. Her daddy carried his rod and reel, a stringer, and the tackle box. He handed her another smaller rod and reel and the fish net. She had only been allowed to fish with bamboo poles and bait up until this point, so she was anticipating being able to work with the beautiful lures in his tackle box. She had her eye on a white lure with orange markings for a long time. They crept down the hill. Her dad went first to make sure she was not going to topple as they wended their way through the growth and roots, and she was glad she was wearing blue jeans. As they came down the riverbank, she saw a world so enchanting her eyes teared up. The light was coming through the trees on all sides, brightening the leaves and the water like a movie set. Tree branches and vines bent down, dripping into the water. A mist rose off the river. As they reached a ledge close to the water, they sat down. No words were spoken.

A large man and a little girl.

They were quiet for a long while—just watching—listening to the bird sounds, maybe a whippoorwill, maybe a dove, and occasionally a splash letting them know it would be a good morning for fishing.

"This is why I come to the Hill Country," Daddy said.

She felt that she'd been let in on a great secret. The world back up the river road was dull and boring and now she'd been allowed to see this slice of beauty.

Daddy went back to the car, telling her, "Girl, sit tight here; don't move an inch."

Alone in this piece of nature, she thought, "I'm gonna remember this when I'm grown-up." She didn't know then that this would be their last whole family vacation. But she knew her mother was dying.

Daddy came back with the coffee and they sat, drinking. It was delicious and warming. She realized for the first time how the chill of the morning and being tired added to the experience. She enjoyed this shivering, but she was glad she had on a long-sleeve shirt and the coffee. She would always love coffee now, she thought.

Finally, Daddy started to get their gear ready. He opened his tackle box and handed her the flashlight to shine in it. Although she loved to look in his tackle box at home in the garage, the colorful lures seemed like treasures down here in this new world. He picked out two.

"These will do the job," he said and put one on his rod and reel and a smaller one on hers. Then, as he had done many times before with her bamboo pole and as he would do many times in the future with a rod and reel, he got her all set up.

Daddy took her near a sitting place he had found on a high part of the ledge and helped her to get her stance. He showed her patiently how to loosen the line in the reel into soft loops in her hand, and how to throw it out with a graceful arc into the water. The sound of it softly plopping into the silky smooth river soothed her. He held his large, round hands around hers and demonstrated what she might feel if a fish seized this opportunity. Then he asked, "All set, Rob?" and to her nodding, moved back and got his own gear in place a few yards away.

He gave her a short lecture on what to do when she felt the pull. Then he demonstrated—reeling in as if there was a pull or to check to see if anything had happened. Daddy cast out his rod several times, getting arranged, and then they were two quiet figures on the river's edge. The waiting was real fine. She could wait there forever.

Daddy felt a pull first, and then his line went just under the water. He reeled in a fine river catfish. He told her to get the fish stringer out of the tackle box and, in the dim light, showed her how to get the wriggling fish off the hook and hold it while he got the loop of the stringer through its cheek. She loved holding something alive even though it was slimy and its fins scratched her. He hooked the stringer around a branch near the bank and lowered the fish into the water to keep it breathing until they left.

Several times she felt her line had gone under, but she reeled in with nothing.

Daddy said, "That's alright. It takes a while to get the feel of what's happening underwater, Roberta."

Maybe this was about things you couldn't see but just have to feel. After watching how he kept casting out, she did that herself, finally catching the line on a tree behind herself.

He came over and wordlessly untangled her, and when she was all set again, he says, "What do you think? Isn't this good?"

And she had to admit, "It's great."

They had an unspoken agreement that it wasn't about catching anything or failing. It was all good.

He got a fish she couldn't see very well in the morning light and threw it back in as too small. Then he caught a couple of good-sized river trout. Finally, she caught a too-little fish as well and managed to get it off the hook and thrown back in all by herself. They continue this unplanned catch and release with little fish until the sun was truly up. Then they packed up and drove back to the cabin. All the way on the ride back, she felt proud. She was a fisherman.

She told herself she wouldn't tell Rita that because she might laugh. When they reached the cabin, Daddy said that he was going to make a big breakfast outside on the fire pit: bacon, eggs, potatoes, and more coffee.

"It just tastes a whole lot better from out here, Rob," he said. He said that she could go in and sleep until it was ready and then he would wake them all up.

But she said, "I can help you, Daddy."

He said, "Okay, Rob, you can stay with me."

They exchanged looks that told them what they felt underneath the surface, and she stayed.

Twelve

The White Blouse
1952

THEY ALL HAD to go—only Roseglen in person could procure her paycheck from the county courthouse. With all of her medical expenses, the money was needed. Her husband, Bob, always drove the family. His mother-in-law flanked his wife's door. Rita and Roberta fussed in the backseat. They were dressed in pinafores with sandals, and still they were burning up. Their little faces dripped with sweat. They waved Sunday school fans with ads on them over each others' faces, creating a little air. A small portable window air conditioner sat in the front window of the car. It blew only warm air in this extreme heat. The sun shone down on the brush country, the cactus, the mesquite trees, and the ocotillo. They all looked thirsty, done in. The sun beat down on the black car. This was the usual in this South Texas desert: stifling heat, hot like a fire. A family in their black Ford, driving home from Laredo.

Suddenly, Roseglen fought, moved around, agitated, grabbing frantically at her clothes. "I can't stand this anymore. I cannot breathe at all."

Red blotches crawled up her face and neck. She wheezed and coughed. She pushed at the dashboard with her hands and the seat back with her head to get away from between her husband and her mother.

An emphysema attack had overcome her. She appeared to be smothering from claustrophobia within her own body, her disease wanting to strangle her. Dressed properly in going-to-town clothes—silk hose, garter belt, slip under a white long-sleeved silk blouse, and a calf length skirt of blue rayon with black low slung pumps—she looked trapped. She pulled and strained at all of these. Her eyes stared off; a frown formed on her face. She became more like a frightened wild animal than a grown woman unbuttoning the silk white blouse she wore. It was cloying, sticking to her skin with perspiration as though she must be rid of it, rid of all of this.

Robert pulled over, she thought to assist.

Instead he said, "Lord's sake, honey, cars will go by. People will see you."

She peers quizzically at the man who usually went to any length to assist her through her painful times. She looks shocked. "You care about strangers in passing cars? You? What is happening to you, Robert?" she wheezed. "You are crossing a line! This isn't you."

Instead of backing down, he got louder. "It could be the neighbors, anyone, people we know. Rose, please, please!" He breathed heavily.

They were both panting now. She saw he was more concerned about how this looked than how she felt. She pulled harder on the sleeves to disentangle herself from the blouse.

Her mother helped her out of it. "Robert, she is choking here! Can't you see that? Do you want to kill her?" Her mother held the limp blouse carefully across her two hands, stared at it as though it is a holy cloth, as though it would give her answers.

Roseglen's world fell topsy-turvy. Usually, her mother Reta admonished all of them to act properly. Now it was her husband in that role, he who loved her more than anyone could possibly love another human being. This upside-down feeling added to her sense of smothering. She didn't care who saw.

Now she knew the truth for sure: She was done for.

The girls saw from the backseat their mother, her torso in only a slip, twisting and turning between the two angry people, the two who cared the most about her and who were fighting over her. They pressed their hot little bodies together, side by side, staring. They had never seen their mother in this undressed state but everything was changing now.

Roseglen protested. "I want out of the car now. You can't keep me here." This was a challenge; she wanted to see if Bob would take up the gauntlet, if he would continue to argue.

She started to climb over the back of the front seat. The girls wanted to help. They had no idea how. Should they take a hold of her arms, now hanging limp over the seat? Gather her sticky red hair, which had preceded her head over the seat back, falling damply close to their hands? In fear of hurting her, they pulled back in anguish from their mother, their mother who desperately needed help. They cowered together, their hot little bodies pushed back into the warm upholstery.

Their grandmother had gotten out of the car. They saw her standing with one hand supporting her bent body on the open car door, shaking her head slowly. Their mother twisted around and climbed out to join her mother. The two women looked into each other's eyes. Roseglen fought the air with her hands and staggered away from the car, away from her mother. She wobbled in her high-heeled pumps down the gravelly side of the road. Bob watched her moving away, off the road, up top only her slip. She walked into the desert. Low cactus plants and mesquite bushes reached for her legs. Everything glowed white in the sunlight. Robert put his head down on the steering wheel, which his hands grasped tightly. He was trying to pray their way out of this. The girls wondered if he, too, was getting ill. They were quiet like stones, frozen in this hot hell.

Until now, they had never seen their parents argue. The main vision they had was of Roseglen sitting in their father's lap, laughing and talking, their mother held in their father's arms. They had seen him at her side, at her beck and call, for months now. He held her in the night when she had an attack; he did all of the serving and picking up around the house when Florinda went home at night. He brought her what she wanted, always—

books, cigarettes, cold cream, avocados, cold Cokes. He placed the oxygen mask over her face when she couldn't get oxygen from the air around her. He lay next to her long, thin body in bed, quietly conversing for hours each night. Very late, the girls heard only his voice—now reading the words in her books to her. They knew then that she was too weak to talk or to hold the book. But she still craved the words, the stories.

He slumped against his car door, then opened it, and stumbled out. He shuffled over to his wife. They were far away where the girls couldn't hear what he said to her; his head was down close to her face. Both faces were dripping with perspiration. Neither face showed anger now. They saw his arms go patiently around her. He guided her gently back to the car, his hand stroking her back, her head resting on his chest.

He quietly asked their grandmother, "Gran, would you get in the back with the girls? She needs the space now." He gave her a look, as though imploring her to obey.

Reta Ingersoll knew this was one time to do what she was asked. She minded her son-in-law. He gingerly helped Roseglen into the front seat and got equipment out of the glove box. The girls knew he was giving their mother an injection. Her head was back, resting, lolling on the headrest. His only words were, "So be it." Then he started the car up and they drove silently home.

Everything had changed.

That night Rita heard short bursts of their parents' conversation. "Sweetheart, I was so scared." "I couldn't breathe." "I felt helpless. I lost perspective on what was important, Rose." "I know, honey, I know. I lost it too." Rita heard what sounded like sobbing, two people crying together. She waited a long while in the dark, listening for it to stop. Then Rita started to the bathroom. Tiptoeing by her parents' bed, she saw their two sleeping heads lying angled together, their cheeks wet, stained with their tears. She forgot about the bathroom, headed back to her and Roberta's room, and slipped into her bed quietly. She didn't make a sound. She did not want Roberta to wake. She wanted to keep her sister from that scene in the other room. Maybe she could protect Roberta from knowing the end was soon, because today on the road from Laredo, they saw plenty of the future their family had crossed into. She whispered aloud, "Plenty enough."

Alone, sitting at the dining room table in her house where she had sat reading her Bible, preparing for Sunday school, Reta Ingersoll wrote of the day to her sister, Ethel. She had gone back home to Nebraska City only once after the divorce, when Bob Ingersoll took her in their new Packard so she could show off how well off they were doing from the oil business, her with the fancy clothes and jewelry, him with the car. All of the family had welcomed her, but they had acted uncomfortable with her wealth. However, Ethel told her that she thought of her daily and missed her as much as she had that night Reta left with the two brothers in the wagon. Reta felt a twinge of guilt then and had vowed to keep the relationship with Ethel alive and to put some honesty into it. She had tried to seem of a different class on that visit. But no matter that Bob had had some success back then, they still lived in a rough part of the world that civilization had bypassed. She had vowed to be more honest with Ethel than she had been on that visit. Sitting at the table that night she thought over the day and her life:

My Dearest Ethel,

Some time has passed since I have written to you, as truth be told, life has become quite hard here in the south of Texas. With Bob's passing, I am struggling with monies and sometimes even have to depend upon Roseglen and Robert for assistance. I sold some of the oil rights Bob Ingersoll owned in order to keep up, but I have been told that might not have been wise. But I manage even in these difficulties. I do not wish for you to worry about me.

However, I must let you know of the heartbreak which is now occurring in my life. That Russian Jewish doctor, Dr. Malakoff, has told Roseglen that she has only a few months to live from her emphysema. You know I have no prejudices, but I insisted that she go to the clinic in San Antonio to confirm this news, and, unfortunately, it is true. I sit here at her table at night and worry and ponder our future. Today on our trip home from Laredo, she had a spell and wandered into the brush. It was the hardest day we've ever had.

I will always help with the girls, but I am growing old. I worry about my own physical well-being. Roseglen has asked me if I will live with Robert Smith and her girls after she passes. It seems an awfully strange arrangement. He and I have been at odds often, but today I saw how much he cares for my daughter. I might see her way to do Roseglen's bidding. He and I will bear the same loss. We both will have our life's love ripped away. It's odd to feel a kinship with him now. You'll remember how I railed against their marriage. Circumstances make changes come upon one.

I don't know if you'll understand what I need to share with you now, but often when I think of her life, it seems more like a fiction, a made-up story. I don't, and haven't for all of these years since leaving Nebraska, felt as though I live in the real world. Nebraska City was civilization. Here, people are unmannered, and we don't have all of the niceties of life. For all of this time, we've had to make those things up. All the ladies and men who had some little talent would gather in the town meeting hall, a tin shack that became the Legion Hall, and provide entertainment, playing our different and usually incompatible instruments and singing. We were just amateurs, and we couldn't raise the cultural level of anyone. Although I enjoyed playing my slide guitar with the singing, I longed for professionals to entertain us. And so it went, with lecturers coming to town. They were most often con artists, never people helping us to learn. We needed something to take us beyond the survival level of our lives. I helped create the school and the church, so you know they couldn't really have been much, as I have no background or skills in that. We sent Roseglen away to boarding school.

We all made things up as we went along, and that's why it feels unreal. All the times I wrote to you before, I was embellishing my life so it would sound grand. It has always been a struggle, Ethel, and I ask your forgiveness.

Watching my daughter strangle for air and breath has brought me to a new and more honest awareness. I promise that my next letter will be more uplifting and not untruthful.

Again all of her love,

Your faithful sister, Reta Glenn

Reta Ingersoll and her sister, Ethel, 1940

Thirteen

Books from the Laredo Public Library
1952

IT BECAME A weekly practice, almost ceremonial—two little girls and their father slowly climbing the steps to the Laredo Public Library. The library was in the center of town, by the city park, on the second story of the Laredo City Office Building. Their visit was a necessity, like air, like breathing.

Each Saturday, Bob Smith took his daughters to town. Going to "town" meant driving to Laredo, the nearest large city. Rita was nine, and Roberta was still seven. They went without their mother, Roseglen, whose illness had progressed to the point where she was always in bed, close to the oxygen tank. Coughing fits, struggling for breath, and blood-filled Kleenex were common accompaniments to her days. These days were surely waning, drawing to a close.

Nevertheless she read. And read and read. Usually, Roseglen covered ten books a week, but sometimes it was more—eleven, thirteen. It is a necessity, a lifeline. Having always been a reader, she now read as if she needed to read to cross over, to get across the River Styx. She had told her girls that myth, leaving them both puzzling over whether their mother actually thought that would be helpful to them as they crossed into a life without her. The girls didn't discuss this; they only exchange looked. Discussing death would somehow bring it nearer. Ignoring it was better, somehow a barrier.

And so the weekly trip to Laredo—to buy groceries, pick up prescriptions, and eat at the Border Café—always ended with the trip to the library. The girls each had to carry a pile of books carefully up the stairs. Later in life, Roberta wondered how they had looked.

Rita went first, climbing purposefully and gracefully. Roberta came next, several steps behind, with a smaller pile but awkwardly grasping the large books, wavering on several steps. She felt gratitude that her father, who came last with the bulk of books, never hurried her or made her feel that she was not up to this task. They all knew the importance of this job, both for Roseglen's hunger for words and for their need to have a task that felt as though they were being helpful in easing the burden of Roseglen's dying. Nothing else was helpful. The little weekly parade of book carriers might have been beneficial to their mother, slow the process. Step, rest, step, rest, look behind, step, rest.

That Saturday, as they'd approach the Border Café, where for many years they ate their Saturday lunch, there were angry-looking men holding signs that said, "We are paid 2 cents an hour to wash dishes. We are men, too."

Never one to cause trouble, their father suddenly but quietly said to the girls, "Let's go to the City Drug Café instead. Your mother always liked that." Rita wished he would not speak of her in the past tense.

They turn around and walked silently down Matamoros Street for a couple of blocks and then crossed the plaza to the City Drug Café. They sat in a booth where Roberta caressed the black glass tabletop, just in case her mother's handprint was somehow still there in spite of the many washings with grey-colored dishcloths. The décor was black, something Roseglen had told the girls was to make the café look sophisticated.

It was only when they were seated that Rita asked, "Why did we leave, Daddy?"

Bob Smith cleared his throat and looked around the café, searching for what, the girls don't know. "Those men were illegal. The men your grandmother feeds sometimes. She calls them wetbacks because they've swum across the Rio Grande from

Mexico. They have come to Texas, to the United States, looking for work."

Several months earlier, the family had seen a truckload of migrant workers in Laredo.

"Look there, girls," Daddy had directed the girls and pointed. "Those trucks are full of families, mothers, daddies, children, even some grandparents. They are Mexican people who are following the crops."

"Where, where, Daddy?" Rita asked. "Where are they going?

"To Michigan to pick beets or to Idaho to shear sheep."

"Is it a long way, Daddy, a very long way?" Roberta asked. "Is it as far as where Grandmother-in-Arkansas lives?"

"Farther, much farther, girls. See this well. These are cattle trucks, filled not with cows and bulls but with people. It will be gone some day. I hope. You are seeing something similar to concentration camps where the girl died in that book your mother read you. It isn't the same, but it's close."

Their mother had joined in. "I hope it is gone someday. I truly wish for that. Anne Frank. She was the girl I read to you about, girls. The Jews were put into train cars. Your Daddy's right. These trucks and those cars are very much alike. The people are packed in, standing, with no bathrooms, no seats." Some of her students and their parents could be in that truck, right there. That's why there are only a few students in her school until October when the work is finished. In Aguilares, there are very few people at home now.

"I remember, Mother. The book frightened me. They had nothing to eat. They ate a horse that was dead in the street. Could that happen to us? Don't let it. Don't let it!" Rita pleaded.

Roberta had whispered, "Could Juan be in that truck, Mother?"

"Dear, I'm sorry to have to say yes but he could be. That little boy whose head you can barely see at the back could be her third grader and your old classmate, Juan. And we have no way of knowing if it could happen to us. When people have what is called prejudice, they do bad things to others. They do it because of people's beliefs or the color of their skin."

Their father told them, "Mexican people are not allowed to eat in many restaurants in Texas. We try not to eat at a restaurant that has that kind of set up. Mexicans can only get low paying jobs. Those things are not right, girls. Each man is a human. As Ma Joad said, 'We are the people.'" He'd looked at their mother when he said this so they knew it was something between them that they wouldn't understand until much later.

"Each person is a human, men, women, and children," their Mother offered. Later they would know that she was preparing them for when she was gone.

There were four trucks in a row in the lane next to them, loaded with standing humans. The trip they took to Arkansas each summer to see their Daddy's family took three days. This was a longer trip for these humans. Two little girls saw injustice for the first time.

Now their father continued explaining what they had seen today, "Places like the Border Café know they can pay them almost nothing, so those men were having what is called a strike. I will never cross a picket line, which is what that is. Although South Texas workers have not and probably never will unionize in her lifetime, I support those who fight for the rights of workers. If I cross their line, I am not in support of their rights as humans."

Roberta was surprised that Rita didn't ask more questions. She didn't understand and was frightened by what had happened. She knew that if her mother were there, she would have continued the conversation, helping the girls to grasp what was obviously an important situation. She had noticed that a man who had just crossed the line had yelled at their father when he turned them around, "Are you yeller, mister?" Bob Smith had simply ignored him, kept the girls walking on. Roberta knew then that from now on she would have to do a lot of figuring out of things on her own.

Mexican men who crossed over illegally knew that their grandmother's house was one where they could find solace and food. The solace came from the pastoral yard she had created with oleanders and lilacs and large salt cedars that, incidentally, provided a hiding place for them near the chicken house in the backyard. There was a table that couldn't be seen from the road where she would serve them leftover food. They weren't privileged to the information that her granddaughters had, which was that Reta Ingersoll had a separate set of old, usually cracked dishes that she washed in an outside washtub after the men ate and then replaced in the chicken house on shelves near the door. She would retrieve them after a gaggle of men approached her back door asking for food and then fill them with the large amounts of leftovers she usually had on hand.

She always answered these men in the affirmative but added admonitions of "Don't linger," and "Please leave all of the plates and silverware on the table." She felt this gave her some control over a situation that she hadn't been able to allow until after her husband's death. "Never speak to wetbacks or give them food or let them near the house," Bob Ingersoll had always told her. Reta knew full well that women on the frontier were the ones left at home when the men went off hunting or to war or some other gallivanting event. Women had a history of having to deal with whoever showed up. She'd had to do this back in Wyoming. Therefore, she had some know-how in these situations. She felt it was her small rebellion from Bob Ingersoll. She also felt that since the men knew she would help, they would be less likely to rob or rape or do evil to her.

This day, the librarian, who was always very gracious to the Smiths, was even more so. She put her arm around each girl and then embraced Bob Smith. The girls had never seen her do this with other patrons. She stood in her prim tailored suit, glasses held on a pin on her jacket, grasping a list of books. Then she asked Bob how Roseglen was doing, and he immediately sent the girls away to the children's section. From there, they could see the two in a quiet, private conversation that was longer and more intense than usual. Today, they were whispering instead of using the quiet voices usually used in the library. Their daddy glanced over at the girls. Rita wondered if now the librarian knew more about their mother's state than they did. "Maybe," she thought, "that was good—the not knowing. Maybe we don't need to know more just now." She looked over at Roberta, who was busily looking through books. She felt a rush of love for her sister and didn't want her to know if the end was coming nearer. She joined Roberta, asking her what she was reading. Roberta didn't look at Rita. She simply said, "I'm reading a book about elves. I like elves." Before she could catch herself, Rita blurted out, "You've never liked elves. You don't really care now what you are reading." Then Roberta looked at her. They exchanged a silent understanding and both thumbed meaninglessly through books. Sitting at a table that caught the sun coming in the windows above, they wondered why the sun kept on shining when they were so sad.

But Roberta had usually felt good there. She liked the quiet stillness of the library. She remembered the first time her mother brought her and Rita to this place filled with books. She had liked the smell of the room and recognized that papery smell whenever she opened a book. She had been amazed that they could take books home and that her mother was always allowed to take as many books as she wanted, although the librarian had told them the general rule was only three books per person. Roseglen was an exception even before her illness because she was such a voracious reader. The librarians asked her for little reviews that they could pass on to other readers, a task she enjoyed.

The librarian helped Bob Smith pick out books for his wife. She'd made a list beforehand which she grasped in her pale fingers.

She knew Roseglen's interests well, and this was one of the more important tasks she had in her career as keeper of books.

Then the three patrons reversed their Saturday procession down the steps of the library. The three book carriers were going home. If you saw them, you'd think their procession of three was sweet. You might not sense the ache of it all.

In the usual way, on the thirty-mile drive home in their black Ford, Rita sat in the front seat with her dad, proudly assuming some of the role of mother. She had a scarf tied around her head and she rolled her window down, a grown-up gesture, the scarf blowing a little in the wind. Roberta sat alone in the back seat, which didn't bother her one bit. Her mother wasn't there, but the books were.

For the months they'd had to provide their mother with her reading material, Roberta felt privileged to sit with her mother's books in the back seat and examine them. She would pick out one, open it in the middle, and sniff its pages. Each had its own scent. Then she'd read a little and examine the title and author. She never questioned why a dying woman would read books of poetry, books about art, and usually a Steinbeck or a Hemingway novel. But the books by Erskine Caldwell surprised her. Roberta knew those were full of questionable people because the book jacket sported women with low-cut blouses and men with bottles of whiskey, and sometimes hugging and kissing was going on in broad daylight. Another anomaly was Emily Post's books on etiquette. Those were things Roberta's grandmother, Reta Ingersoll, cared deeply about. Did her mother really need to know the proper placement for silverware on the dinner table at this juncture in her life? And why would she concentrate on unsavory people if she was going to heaven? Although Roberta wasn't sure she herself believed in heaven, she thought that even though her mother didn't, it would still be best if her mother behaved in a way to ensure her entry there, just in case.

It would be years before Roberta would wonder what she herself would want to read at the end of her own life. In that moment, though, she liked knowing what her mother was reading. A few years later, she wondered if she would want something related to church or something funny or something about the world around her, animals, bugs, grasses, trees? Many years later, she knew that she'd want to read poetry, stories, books about jungles, art, and travel. Death, she mused then, was a kind of travel, wasn't it?

It was also many years and experiences later that Roberta realized that her mother's fondness for Erskine Caldwell helped her daughter to know there was a sexual side of life. She liked to think that her mother knew Roberta looked over the books; that she knew she'd miss helping her daughters grow from childhood to adulthood. Maybe they'd want to read Caldwell when they were older and from their readings could glean some of what that adolescent crossing would entail.

Roberta didn't have a single memory of her parents ever going out as a couple. Her friends talked of their parents going out dancing at honky-tonks or even nightclubs. But the closest Roseglen and Bob Smith came was their Sunday evening ritual.

The whole family would clamber into the car for a short ride to Oilton for hamburgers. The car was, of course, a Ford because a relative by marriage was a Ford salesman in Laredo. Sometime in the year before her mother's passing, they got a new car. Rita and Roberta, who knew phone calls were ripe for getting news, heard their dad talking to that relative, Don Love. They heard him mention a car radio. They were delighted and clapped hands and spun around the room until they were told to stop making themselves dizzy. And sure enough, when Daddy drove home with the car late Saturday, their new green 1952 Ford had a radio. This made the drive ten miles to Oilton, a town much smaller than Mirando City, really special. They listened to a country station on the way there and a top hits station on the way home.

Roberta guessed later that this was to accommodate their parents'
differing tastes in music, but at the time that did not occur to her.
Their parents rarely disagreed.

The destination on Sunday evening was Charlie O'Jedas
drive-in burger place. It was not a drive-in with carhops, roller
skates, or window trays. Their daddy had to drive their car close
enough to the front window of Charlie's narrow falling down
unsigned building to bang on the window until Charlie appeared.
Daddy would ask how he was "doin' nowadays," order two bags
of Eight for a Dollar Hamburgers and fries all around. Then they
would wait there while Charlie cooked and handed the bags out.
Daddy would tip his hat, say "Much obliged," and they'd pull
around to the other side to eat. Their dad always got a side of
jalapenos and popped a few during his meal. He would eat seven
or eight burgers, and the "women," as he jokingly called them,
would eat two or three apiece. They were perfectly greasy, loaded
with cheese, tomatoes, onion, and lettuce, all the fixin's. It was
Roberta's favorite meal out, much easier than the Border Café in
Laredo, where there were so many decisions and manners were
required. Sitting in their own car, in the dark, no one reminded
the girls to close their mouths while chewing or to eat all of their
food. No one had to. The burgers were that good. On the way
home, Daddy would say, "This world and then the fireworks!"
Rita imagined a beautiful sky after death.

After the ride home listening to Patti Page and Tony Bennett,
Rita and Roberta would hastily bathe and then join their parents,
now seated on the green flowered davenport, his arm around her,
and in Roberta's memory, her arm draped over his legs, in a very
cuddly manner. Rita and Roberta would pounce onto the floor in
front of them. Frank Sinatra would already be singing, and early
on, both girls sensed a different mood in their parents on these
nights. They unknowingly understood this was their parents'
romantic time. Roberta didn't know if their parents didn't have
the inclination or the energy or the money for going out, but she

was secretly glad. Later in life, she was pleased to have seen this when friends told her that they had never even seen their parents kiss or hug. When Frank sang "You Do Something to Me," the adults would occasionally lean in to each other for a long kiss followed by a few short sprinkles of kisses. As the evening wore on, their mother's head would be nestled on their father's shoulder. Rita and Roberta understood this was something for grown-ups, maybe romance, maybe love. It was very natural and comfortable. The evening, or at least Rita and Roberta's part in it, invariably ended when they would all sing "Good Night, Irene" along with Frank. It was their Sunday night bedtime song.

> Irene good night, Irene good night,
> Good night Irene, good night Irene,
> I'll see you in her dreams.
>
> Last Saturday night I got married,
> Me and her wife settled down,
> Now me and her wife we are parted,
> I think I'll go out on the town.
>
> Sometimes I live in the country,
> Sometimes I live in town,
> Sometimes I take a great notion
> To jump in the river and drown.
>
> I love Irene, God knows I do,
> I'll love her 'til the seas run dry,
> But if Irene should turn me down,
> I'd take morphine and die.
>
> Stop rambling, stop your gambling,
> Stop staying out late at night,
> Go home to your wife and your family,
> Stay there by your fireside bright.

The Erskine Caldwell books were about poor whites, and if someone was not acting properly, a member of the Smith family might admonish, "Don't act like you're from *Tobacco Road*," one of his famous books. When they were older, Roberta and Rita would learn that Caldwell's books were extremely lurid but also denouncements of racism and mistreatment of the poor. Then they understood better the complexity of their mother, a woman who loved Erskine Caldwell and Emily Dickinson, both at once.

Years later Bob Smith took his daughters for an epic movie at the Plaza Theatre in Laredo where they often retreated after shopping trips for the air-conditioning before the hot drive to Mirando City. They went to see Giant. Rita and Roberta commented to each other quietly that they were the only Anglos in the theatre. They were uncomfortable and yet rooting for the Mexicans when they were refused service in a café and James Dean stood up for them. The event repeated itself for Roberta years later in Detroit when she with her husband sat in a theatre watching Melvin Peebles movie, *Watermelon Man* and the black audience, angry throughout as the movie showed those same unfounded prejudices toward blacks. By then she was clear on where she stood on prejudice but again wasn't quite sure they were welcome in the theatre.

Arriving home from the library in the dusk of that late afternoon, the trio again traipsed in a line from the car, carrying the stories into the house to be lined up with the piles of bought books that had gathered in the front hall since all bookshelf space was full.

Then Bob prepared Roberta's favorite meal, breakfast for dinner, waffles and bacon, and the three ate a quiet meal in the kitchen. You could hear clinking silverware and the slurping of milk. No one talked. Tonight the food didn't even taste good; it didn't taste like anything because Roseglen hadn't felt hungry. They didn't carry her food and their plates into her bedroom to perch on the bed as they usually did, including her in their meal.

Afterward, though, Roseglen said she felt good enough for the girls to bring her the new books to peruse. Rita and Roberta eagerly brought them in, making several trips to her bedside. Then each one sat on either side of their mother, occasionally lightly leaning their heads onto her bed-jacketed arms. The girls tried to not look at the oxygen tank and the many pill bottles on the side table. Their father sat on the dresser stool. Meanwhile, Roseglen picked out a book to read. This time it was Steinbeck's *Of Mice and Men*. She read the opening lines to the girls.

"A few miles south of Soledad, the Salinas River drops in close to the hillside bank and runs deep and green. The water is warm, too, for it has slipped twinkling over the yellow sands in the sunlight before reaching the narrow pool."

As she read, both Rita and Roberta had in their minds' eyes the Frio River where they went to the cabin by Leakey each summer to fish and swim in the sunlit pools. Roseglen pictured that same spot and tried to burn it into her memory. She knew she wouldn't go back there, so she pictured Bob and the girls without her, frolicking on the banks of the Frio.

And then, between coughing fits and efforts to catch her breath, Roseglen kissed her girls and sent them off to bed.

Fourteen
All Along
1952

Some keep the Sabbath going to the Church—
I keep it, staying at Home—
With a Bobolink for a Chorister—
And an Orchard, for a Dome—
Some keep the Sabbath in Surplice—
I just wear her Wings—
And instead of tolling the Bell, for Church,
Our little Sexton—sings.
God preaches, a noted Clergyman—
And the sermon is never long,
So instead of getting to Heaven, at last—
I'm going, all along.
— Emily Dickinson, 1860

THEIR MOTHER, ROSEGLEN was sitting on the padded bench in front of her dresser, putting on makeup on Sunday morning. Her negligee and a bed jacket hung off her shoulders. Rita and Roberta were in summer nightgowns in their bare feet. They sat in front of their mother, facing her, in the open space below the large round dresser mirror. They were very attentive. Their eyes widened watching her transformation. She carefully powdered away the freckles on her lovely pale face surrounded by soft red hair. She vigorously brushed her hair and sparks flew out enchanting us. The dresser was covered with makeup accoutrements—round white-flower decorated face-powder boxes with puffs spilling out, red Maybelline mascara boxes, gold lipstick tubes, hand-mirrors, perfume bottles, eye-brow pencils, and sharpeners. Smells and smudges abounded.

Their mother was getting ready for the day, not for church. In a little while, they would be gotten ready for church by their grandmother, Reta Ingersoll. She would dress them in summer pinafores and white sandals with socks, walk them across a bridge to the little white Methodist Church across the way. They would sing hymns and then Reverend Wilson would preach to them. Roberta liked the way the morning light full of dust motes shimmered in through the church windows. She thought there was something holy about it. When she was a teenager, she would be invited to stand up at her classmate Josephine's *quinceañera* celebration at the local Catholic Church, the celebration of a girl turning fifteen. Only Mexicans attended church there. Candles lit the darkness of the altar full of chalices and crosses and linens. An odor which she would come to know as incense, filled the tiny white clapboard church. The ritual took place in Latin. The priest placed the body of Christ right on her tongue. At their church the only smell was fresh flowers. Their grandmother prepared the communion of grape juice and crackers representing the body and blood of Jesus. In their church, the cross was a simple white. At Josephine's, it was rough wood with a bleeding sculpture of Christ hanging loose, head forlorn. At Josephine's church, a stranger in long robes put a wafer into her mouth, making it seem like a parcel of the actual body. Petite little Josephine, who could out dribble any opposing basketballer, was dressed in wedding white. She was going from childhood to womanhood at age fifteen, right in her church. In an innocent way, Roberta did that in the dark of her grandmother's porch in the swing with Rofie.

In a later time, the Methodist Church would become a junk store full of doctor's examining tables, white cabinets, hospital beds, dental equipment. This was about as close as Mirando would come to having a medical facility. Thank goodness their grandmother was not alive then—she would have felt her community was being sacrificed to the heathens, and that it was an indication of what the world was coming to.

On the way to church, their grandmother reminded them that she hoped they would soon accept Jesus as their savior. As the Sunday school superintendent, she had a great desire for her granddaughters to follow in her footsteps. But Roberta might heed a different desire.

Each Sunday during the makeup ritual, their mother talked to them about going to church. "Girls, when you grow up, you can believe what you want and you can even decide whether you want to go to church. Always remember Emily Dickinson's words, "Instead of getting to heaven at last, I'm going all along." I live always by those words. Sitting out in the yard on these mornings when you go to church, I enjoy lots of thoughts and a bobolink always provides the hymns." Rita thought maybe the bobolink knew her favorite hymn "What a Friend I Have in Jesus." That comforted her.

Sitting in that little dresser alcove, Roberta was struck by the care with which their mother pus mascara and eyebrow pencil on her eyes. They loved how she asked them to choose the color of lipstick for the day. They did notice that she gave them only two or three choices although she had many tubes of lipstick. She pressed her newly lipsticked lips on a neatly folded Kleenex which came out with a perfect print. She ended each session with a little perfume, Chanel #5, behind each ear, and then put a little behind their ears. Although the transformation was transient, it added some permanency to their lives. They loved this weekly ritual.

Right then they didn't know the importance of her words. She read Emily Dickinson to them often and they noticed that the poems she read were often about death. Roseglen's father, Bob Ingersoll, died several years before and she didn't go to the funeral. They wondered if the funeral was in a church and that was why she didn't go. Funerals were important events and yet she stayed home with them.

THEIR MOTHER DIED in April, on Good Friday. All of the neighbor ladies flocked to their house, to comfort the two little girls. Roberta was seven years old and Rita was nine. The ladies told them just go ahead and cry. Roberta decided to never cry in front of any one of them. The ladies told them, "Now your mom is in heaven. She is in a much better place." They didn't discuss this. Rita seemed to grasp this horrific event in their lives better than Roberta. Although she didn't know for sure what her beliefs were, she didn't see how their mother could be in a better place. She asks God each night if he could just let her please talk with her for a little bit. She just needed a little help, a little more reassurance about this whole thing. One of the worst things about all of this was that Daddy's told the girls, "I've let Florinda go, now." He explained it to them one day in the car on the way home from Laredo. He said that they didn't need her any more now that Teacher was moving in with them. Rita didn't understand how he could let a family member go, just go. Their housekeeper was a part of the family. They never mentioned this to him, but at night Roberta and Rita thought of her, too, as they cried for their mother.

They knew their mother didn't go to heaven just at the end; she went all along. She was going to heaven when she woke to Daddy bringing her a cup of coffee in bed; when they watched her putting on makeup; when she sat on their daddy's lap laughing, when she read poetry to them and showed them art prints, when she taught in her one-room school, when she sat talking with her friend Dorothy, when she lit the Salem cigarettes with the classy cigarette lighter their Daddy had given her, when she read her books late into the night, and when she drove them to her school in the early dark, talking with them.

Fifteen
The Sleeping Porch
1954

"I KNOW IT'S late," their Daddy told Aunt Ruth who answered the door. It was eleven at night. They'd driven down the Valley, to San Benito, to Ruth and Buster's. Buster was Daddy's brother and Daddy lived with him and Ruth for several years growing up, away from his mother after his daddy died and things were tough.

Ruth laughed. "No matter, Bob. You are always welcome. This is your home." Their Daddy quoted back to her a poem Roseglen taught him: "Home is where you go and they have to take you in." This made Roberta feel even more like an orphan, that horrid word, Rita's friend Patsy called them after their mother's death.

Ruth took them out to the sleeping porch at the back of the house and Rita and Roberta made the night right there, camping on daybeds pushed together. They quickly undressed into summer nightgowns and lay listening to the cicadas, the sprinklers and watch the shadows of palm trees on the screened in porch. They were the dominant growth in this lush "Oasis of the Valley, the belly of South Texas" as their uncle who was a farmer liked to call it.

Their Daddy hadn't paid any mind to the sleeping habits of a farmer or Ruth's commitment to the early blush of dawn. He was farther outside propriety now than he ever was and he wasn't ever very far in it.

The girls lay stock still under the cedar chest smell of the sheets, listening to Daddy, Aunt Ruth, and Uncle Buster, their voices, their murmurs. Daddy, the newly widowed one, gave the news of his situation, telling what life without Roseglen, his sweetheart, their mother, had brought on. Roberta saw in her mind's eye their mother sitting on his lap, him watching her brush her red hair in the early morning, sparks flying off. Then he was standing, drinking coffee, carefully considering the tall redhead dressed in her nightgown with sleeping jacket, his head filled with reverence.

In the girls' memory that night, they only heard sounds, mutes, gutturals, an occasional stop, a muffled laugh, but they got the gist. They were to be pitied, taken care of or taken in whenever and wherever they showed up. They had slipped out of normalcy and had no more routine. As though they had a routine for the months of coughing and oxygen tanks and blood on Kleenex and rushed trips to the hospital ending in long, drawn-out stays. They'd always thought that would end and they would go back to usual. But here they were. A fluorescent light flickered at the other end of the porch. A mosquito buzzed. Rita was sound asleep, beginning to ignore whatever wasn't to her liking. Roberta was wide-awake, taking it all in.

Sixteen

The Doctor's Wife
1954

HOUSES IN SMALL towns had lives, personalities. The spirits of families inhabited these houses for generations. One such house in Mirando City was the Stanley house.

It was a long white house and it belonged to Mrs. Stanley, a widow. Locals called it a "shotgun house" because you could stand at the front door and shoot straight out the back, as each room unfolded into the next and so on. Their daddy told Rita and Roberta that houses were built like that so that if a husband surprised his wife with another man as soon as he entered, he could shoot the intruder as he fled out the back door.

Mrs. Stanley was an older woman who dressed herself in layers. Her costume consisted of shift, blouse, vest, scarf, silk wrap, long skirt, overskirt, gloves, and hat. Yes, a hat even in South Texas in the 1950s. Her outfits floated around her oversized body. Her soft face was made up of white layers of powder, lips jumped out of it. She obviously applied her makeup with a shaking, overly generous hand.

Years after their mother died, their father moved, with his new wife, into Mrs. Stanley's house, leaving them behind with their grandmother. The second room in the line of rooms had been Doctor Stanley's dispensary and Roberta hoped it would be full of Mrs. Stanley's husband's medical instruments to explore on their visits there. She searched for tools, poking and prodding or maybe magical drugs. But, no, it was empty. Still, she could feel the doctor's spirit there.

Louise was their father's new wife. A year or so before she arrived, one day when their Daddy was at work, the girls slipped into his room. They opened the narrow top drawer of the big dresser he had inherited from his mother. They had a habit of going through Daddy's or Teacher's dressers and closets whenever they were left home.

It had become an ordinary practice. Maybe they were looking for something, hints, and memories of their mother, some ephemera to help them cope. That particular day, they discovered papers in their father's top drawer where ordinarily they encountered socks, underwear, ties, containers of cuff links, old wallets, etc. There was a letter from a woman to Daddy. They turned to the signature. The name was Spanish sounding. The letter spoke of waiting for him to visit and of love. The two girls, now eleven and thirteen, sat close on their father's bed, the chenille bedspread etching into their bare legs in summer shorts. They read the letter together, silently. It was signed, "*Mi amor.*"

Perhaps they were both remembering that on Saturday nights they would hear him getting ready in the bathroom. Water ran for bathing and they heard the tinkering of shaving. Their daddy would come into the living room smelling of Aqua Velva, wearing a suit jacket and a fresh shirt. They hadn't known where he was going but they knew it wasn't to a beer joint. He would only say, "I'm going out. I'll be back later." They always felt a queasiness in their stomachs then. Rita carefully folded the letter and replaced it without a word.

Several months later, their grandmother called them into the living room. Being called into Reta Ingersoll's formal living room was serious. They sat on the footstool. Roberta slid behind Rita, looking for protection. They knew something was brewing. "Girls, I hadn't wanted to bring you into this. But I'm sure you've noticed your father going out most weekends. Recently he has gone to Freer, and I knew it wasn't to see his sister, Willard. I had just a notion it was something else. Finally, last night he asked me to sit down with him at the kitchen table." Roberta could see them sitting together in the dimly lit kitchen. "This is what he said: 'Gran, I want you to know first, before the girls. Willard has introduced me to a wonderful lady, Louise, and I've asked her to marry me. I'm renting the Stanley house, and her things will be moved there next week. We will marry this weekend. You've been a godsend to me, taking care of the girls. Now I don't know what to do with them. Should I take them, or do you want to continue with their caretaking?' You will be glad to know that, of course, I told him I would always take care of you. What I didn't tell him, but I feel compelled to tell you, is that this is wrong. Bob Smith marrying now is wrong. It soils the memory of your mother. I am heartsick and may never get over this, but I will be strong for you."

While Roberta focused on the words "caretaking" and "soils," Rita asked, "When, when is she coming?" Roberta heard in Rita's tone something like the appearance of the wicked witch. Now their father was going away. His words later that night telling how much he would see them and still be there for them were no solace. He'd come home with alcohol on his breath, something that had occurred more often since he'd become a widower. He spoke quickly and his voice shook, "I know Gran told you all her news. I will see you often. I will still be your daddy." They would have to be strong again. Lying in their beds that night, Rita gave Roberta no relief when she said, "At least it isn't that Mexican woman. Think of that in this town!"

Their grandmother forbad them to visit their dad's home after they married the woman. They developed a view of Louise as evil. She had stolen their father. On the rare occasions when they disobeyed and went to their house, Louise told them stories of the big city, where she had lived. She showed them her pretty things, jewelry, photos, souvenirs. They were confounded. She didn't seem as wretched as their grandmother said. It would be ten years later, after Louise's death, they began to see what romantic love could mean. Roberta wrote a letter of apology to their Daddy. He never mentioned it. Maybe it came too late.

Years before their father moved to the Stanley house, and they all still lived in with their grandmother, he would often get calls for assistance from Mrs. Stanley. Bob Smith knew that his girls' mother, now passed on, would want him to assist the woman since she was a widow. When one of them answered the phone, they knew, by her highfalutin', British sounding accent, that it was her. They'd run to get their Daddy after she asked, "May I please have the pleasure of speaking with Mr. Smith?" They'd gotten the idea that they were bothersome. "The Docta and I chose to not have offspring. It was a decision," Mrs. Stanley often said. They did have a little yapping miniature dog of some sort, which she always brought along with her.

They already knew the whole script of the call by heart. Rita and Roberta would sit down on the floor under the dining room table, near their father's feet, enjoying the conversation over and over. The smell of furniture polish filled their noses. They ran their hands up and down the knobby rounded table legs, legs they polished each Saturday. Although Daddy knew they were beneath him on the flowered covered rug, they stayed silent. Mrs. Stanley's voice was breathy, but she spoke loudly. She was probably already a little deaf. Daddy held the receiver out a bit from his ear. They could hear both speakers. They knew that, while her husband had practiced medicine for a while in Mirando, eventually that privilege had been revoked when his prescriptions were untranslatable or clearly inappropriate for the illness. They also knew that for many years until his death, he kept giving out what medicines he had left without the privilege of a medical license. Small towns kept these events as confidences.

"Mr. Smith, how am I finding you today?" Rita would look at Roberta and they would suppress giggles, remembering that the first time they heard this they thought Mrs. Stanley was amazed that these two little girls had the ability to find their dad. Now they knew she was asking about his well-being. "Mrs. Stanley, I'm doing pretty good today. And how are you on this fine day?" he'd respond.

"I am not well at all. I do think you know the main reason for my call. We have to make a plan. I truly need and want you to be the person to take me to Saltillo. You know that was my town, the town in Mexico that the Docta loved. He would not want so many months—years—to have gone by without his bride going back there for a repast."

"Well, Mrs. Stanley, I truly hope to be able to do that someday for you. I truly do. What is it you're wanting from me on this day?"

"I just need to go to the grocery store for a very few items, and I wondered if you could take me this afternoon. Let's say you stop by after the luncheon time. If I answer the door, we'll set out. If I don't answer, you will know that I am indisposed. You may go on about your day."

"Fine, Mrs. Stanley, I'll arrive at your home around one o'clock."

She continued in a whisper, "One more thing, Mr. Smith. I hope your girls are not listening."

Daddy was silent. Like Roberta he didn't like to fib.

"It would be best if the girls didn't come. You know that is why I am childless. I get flustered around very young people."

Their Daddy knew they loved these trips and their presence made them more bearable for him, so he just said, "I'll be seeing you a little later, Mrs. Stanley," as he gently replaced the phone on the receiver. He grimaced a little at the thought of his girls knowing he had cut her off.

These trips happened so frequently that they knew how to prepare the car. They immediately went to get the pillow on the lowest linen shelf. It had a plastic cover, and together they pulled on a fresh pillowcase. They put it on the front passenger seat. Mrs. Stanley always suggested that their Daddy remove the pillow, but he would tell her in a low conspiratorial voice that the girls wanted her to be more comfortable. "If I take it away, their feelings would be hurt."

On one of the first trips, as she got out of the car, Mrs. Stanley had leaned back in and whispered, "Bob, I have a medical condition. I tinkled just a little on your car seat." Then in a louder voice, "I give you my deepest thanks, Mr. Smith," and she was off in her usual flurry, clothes flying, and a powdery smell in her wake.

Mrs. Stanley and other bizarre people in Mirando taught the girls that being unusual isn't a bad thing. They learned that from Mrs. Stanley in spite of her condition. They thought perhaps we all have "conditions."

After they picked up Mrs. Stanley, the best part of the trip happened. It was the reason Roberta relished these short journeys. It was only in her thirties that she gave credit to Mrs. Stanley for her wanderlust. Mrs. Stanley saw their father as the only possibility of one last vacation in Mexico. Therefore, she spent all of the driving time, on the way to the grocery store and the several other stops she added on to the trip, describing Saltillo. Although living near the border, Rita and Roberta had never crossed into Mexico. Mrs. Stanley made it sound enchanting.

Rita was not as enthralled as Roberta was, but she always came along. She came to defend herself. At some point, Mrs. Stanley would bring up another plan she had involving Rita. Mrs. Stanley would ask Daddy to stop the car. He would pull over but still stare out of the front of the car window. This was the only time Mrs. Stanley addressed one of them. She'd turn around, always annoyed if Rita was directly behind her. If Roberta was in the other seat, she stared at her while addressing Rita. "Rita, you may not have noticed, but I am becoming elderly. An unusual part of that for me is that I am afraid at night. Some nights it is terrifying." Her quaking voice now sounded less certain.

Roberta always sneaked a look at Rita at this point in the conversation, as her sister would look bug-eyed and terrified, an unusual face for her. "I was thinking that the Docta would be happy if you would come spend a night with me every once in a while, just for the company. I would not be so afraid." After their Daddy started to turn to her in protest, she would always say, "Now, Bob, let her think about it for herself." Rita and Roberta later discussed how odd it was that she wanted Rita to protect her but otherwise did not want either of them around. They also wondered how the doctor would know any of it, since he was dead.

At this point, Rita would be staring out the window at the dusty streets and the little houses. When Mrs. Stanley made her request, Rita would glare at her face or the back of her head, giving no response. Their dad would then say, "Mrs. Stanley, you know these girls don't have a mother. They need each other at night. And they need me." He said it softly so that she would always reply in the only hesitant voice she used. "I just forgot for a little while, Mr. Smith." Her little dog, Pepi, firm in her lap, always yipped at this point. Rita thought she might have squeezed him to get this result. He could protest if she couldn't.

She went on. "Oh, well, then. . . . Let me tell you a little about Saltillo." This was what I was waiting for. Why I always wanted to go on the errand car rides. Mrs. Stanley began her story.

"Mr. Smith, we would just need to cross into Mexico at Meir and then journey down the Federale Highways 57 and 45 to arrive at the city of waterfalls." The girls liked the way she broke up "Fed er ali." They imitated it later.

They relished the way she spoke. It was different from the other adults they knew, fancy and unusual. A mixture of a British accent and Spanish words. She talked with her hands a great deal. Her soft pudgy very white hands were always moist. Now they both leaned forward, toward Mrs. Stanley's words and hands. But Mrs. Stanley would ignore them. She looked straight ahead and went on.

"Saltillo is known for its perfect climate, *clima*! But being a colonial city, what I admire the most is its heart for learning; it is considered the Athens of Mexico. I've told you before, Mr.

Smith, that Athens, the Greek center of learning, is the model for a perfect civilization. As in Athens, intellectuals—*intelectuales*—gathered in Saltillo in earlier times! That is one of the things that makes living in this town quite tiresome for me. There are few intellectuals here, if any. Your wife, your Roseglen, was one, God rest her soul."

Ignoring that he was excluded from her labeling and quite comfortable with that position, Bob Smith agreed, "She was that. She was very smart."

"And I don't know if I've told you," Mrs. Stanley continued, "that we consorted with artists, musicians, writers, and politicians during our time in Saltillo."

"Oh, yes, Mrs. Stanley, you have told me that," Bob Smith replied without a hint of impatience. Although unsure of its meaning, Roberta loved the word civilization and rolled it slowly in her mouth. She was fairly certain that they did not live in a perfect civilization. She had in fact heard their grandmother refer to South Texas as a "quite uncivilized land." She told them that she had no idea why Bob Ingersoll had brought her to this godforsaken place.

Roberta imagined Saltillo would be the opposite.

Rita and Roberta had to lean back for the next part, to be stabilized for the best part of Mrs. Stanley's description of Saltillo. "What I am drawn to, the thing that makes it my heart's desire to journey back to the place I shared every winter with the Docta, is, naturally"—here she would pause—"its color!"

Rita loved this part.

"Look out the window. Look out." She gestured here toward the buildings they were passing. "Our town, Mirando, is not in color. Not at all! We live in a town that's in shadows, without tints and shades of paint. There's no artist's palette here! But Saltillo . . . Saltillo is like a sensuous painting." As they looked out, following her instructions, they knew it too. And they felt bad about it. The sun beating down and the dust made our town look worn out. They felt sorry for Mirando. Here both Rita and Roberta imagined the paintings their grandfather created after emphysema laid him low, making him unable to keep up with the oil rig business. They saw the blues and oranges and browns he saw in this landscape around him. They wanted to be in a painting. But they waited for her descriptions of the fantasy world of Saltillo.

"The main point I can make to you, Mr. Smith, is that it is a sensuous pearl pink, that is, the buildings are that. And when the sun shines, the pink is everywhere. On the streets, the sky, the people's faces."

As she spoke, Roberta imagined the pink-faced people surrounded by pink sky and pink buildings.

"And oh, oh, oh! There is the Cathedral of Saltillo! It's always on my mind. It appears heavily ornamented with silver hearts and paintings and sculptures. There are many chapels attached to the main aisle. I would go there and light a candle for alleviation of my many troubles. I often lit them for the Docta!"

Then there was silence as Mrs. Stanley drifted off, staring out the window while all of the Smiths give quite a lengthy consideration to her heavy troubles. "I wonder if long ago on a trip with her now-deceased husband, she had been concerned about the doctor's health, or if he caused her trouble throughout their life together," Rita whispered.

After a long pause, where the girls squirmed, she would continue. "But the Park Alameda Zargosa—Mr. Smith, when I speak of it I am like the young woman I was when the Docta first took me there! I am struck by his handsome face, I am almost swooning. This is the most beautiful park in all the western hemisphere, I am certain. Shade trees, flowering bushes, birds, benches, and the fountains—ah, they are everywhere. There was always music, mariachi bands! We would stroll slowly, arm in arm, and even now my heart beats under my ribs with such fervor." Here her voice was low, almost in a whisper. "I tell you, Mr. Smith, such fervor! I do feel quite faint!"

It was at this part in the talk that Roberta knew that she must travel; that she must find a beautiful park and walk arm in arm with someone there. She needed to see cathedrals and fountains and buildings shining with sun.

Then Mrs. Stanley would say, "But there is something of great importance to Saltillo, something of which you know nothing, Mr. Smith!"

The girls felt that she was reprimanding their father for his lack of knowledge about this city, but he graciously asked, "And what ever would that be, Mrs. Stanley?" full well knowing what she was going on to in the next subject of her soliloquy.

"The tiles! This colonial city is decorated with the most beautiful tiles in existence. Azuelos. Because the most beautiful tiles in the world are made right here. Right here in Saltillo." She sometimes slipped into thinking that she and their Daddy were on their journey to her town. "Stories are told in the tiles that cover almost every building we see: restaurants, stores, offices, homes, churches. The tiles are like miniature paintings, and they tell stories of the history and daily life of Saltillo. The whole city is decorated for Christmas all of the time! We are so thrilled by them, Robert."

The girls looked at each other knowingly, punctuating the fact that she now called Daddy by his first name. She was in Saltillo.

Suddenly, they were at Christian's grocery store, a tiny shack with tin advertisements tacked all over its front, the stoop occupied by slouching men and sleeping dogs. When the car stopped, everyone was shocked. They were in Mirando City. The sky was fuzzy blue from the hot sun. There was no pink anywhere. The girls were always dismayed to realize that they were not actually in the enchanted city that Mrs. Stanley had taken them to with her words. Brought back to reality, they would beg their Daddy for a raspa, a lovely shaved ice treat that was Mr. Christan's specialty. They needed something to dress up this unenchanting town we lived in.

As they clambered out of the car, pleading for their treat, Mrs. Stanley would admonish, "Oh, these bothersome youngsters you have acquired, Mr. Smith." They would roll their eyes at each other and follow her and their Daddy into the store.

Eons later, while standing in the Sistine Chapel in Rome or in the Arena Chapel in Padua, Italy, Roberta would think of how Mrs. Stanley's desire to travel had grabbed her on those car trips. The stories still shone out to her like tiles. In her mind's eye, she saw God reaching his hand to Moses on the Sistine ceiling or the Nativity scene in Padua etched on tiles as Mrs. Stanley had seen stories in the streets of Saltillo. The tiles became a part of who Roberta was, her desires.

Roberta read in the Border Beat online that in the twenty-first century, Saltillo was under fire. The focus was off the color and the tiles and on the armed men on the roofs and the gunfire heard in the streets. She was glad Mrs. Stanley didn't live to see this.

Back then, Roberta felt two opposing things: pity for Mrs. Stanley and an admiration for her love of a beautiful town, two thoughts at the same time. She once asked her father if he would ever take Mrs. Stanley to Saltillo. When he said that he couldn't really see his way to do that, she vowed that she would not rely on the kindness of others to enable her travel dreams. She would have a brilliant art historian to walk arm in arm with, but she would be the protagonist in those dreams. Roberta, would seek those tiles in her life.

Seventeen
George Washington's Birthday
1954

THEY MUDDLED THROUGH the holidays. She died on Good Friday. She had picked out their Easter dresses. They didn't remember dying or looking for eggs that first year. On the fourth of July, no one suggested a picnic. In October, Rita and Roberta trick or treated at a few houses until they tired of "Oh, you poor little things," and the extra candy, so they trudged back up their hill.

Roberta thought of her first Halloween when she was two. They put on Daddy's jackets and shoes and were shepherded out the side door to go around to the front door to trick or treat their mother. Roberta fell going down the outside steps in those big shoes and knocked out a tooth, so they just sat on the couch with ice on her mouth, one on each side of their mother, she telling them stories.

On Thanksgiving, they went to Aunt Gracie and Uncle Roland's house because they has no children and they felt like orphans. Aunt Gracie twittered around them as though they were sick. Roberta couldn't take it and went to sit in the car and play the radio. When she finally heard the screaming, calling of her name, their Daddy was about to jump into the cold pond behind the house, thinking Roberta had done herself in.

Christmas was the hardest. Their grandmother and daddy constantly debated all of it.

"Should we have a tree?" Should we have the usual turkey dinner? Had she already bought presents for the girls?" Their mother usually shopped early and the girls spent any time their parents were away, searching the closets for presents. Just ask her. Make this all go away, Roberta wanted to yell.

By February and the biggest celebration of the year in Laredo, George Washington's Birthday, they thought they were ready to try something. They dressed up and piled into the car for the girls' first trip back to Laredo, the town of her death, the place she was buried. This festival was meant to bring together the Dos Laredos, the towns on either side of the border, Anglos and Mexicans together, and the Indians, too.

Rita and Roberta were dead quiet on the ride, with Teacher and Daddy straining to make conversation. "This is a big deal because the first president chopped down a mesquite tree not a cherry tree and he did not do it with an ax. He used a machete. At least that is the Mexican version of it," their Daddy told them. They giggled.

Traffic slowed to a crawl as they entered Laredo. They inched down Benavides Boulevard to Dora's hair salon. Teacher wanted her hair done before going to the parade and their dad and the girls would eat lunch at the bus station café next door. No one wanted to go to the City Drug Café. It was full of their mother. "After hairdos and food, we will all be ready for the parade," Daddy offered hopefully. No one really cared.

The last time they'd gone to the parade was with their mother. She'd pointed out the Lantana Queen, and the most decorated float with George and Martha and the bands, and their favorites, the dancers and mariachi bands from Mexico. The floats were covered in real flowers. Roberta began to feel a dread. Flowers and funerals. Every sight was tainted. Rita whispered, "Why do we bother?" Silently her sister agreed. "Why bother with anything?" her gut told her. They both wanted to slink away, disappear.

The three of them walked slowly into the bus station. Bus stations were lonely places, but it seemed more so today. Everyone was already at the parade. Their Daddy told them that he would order at the counter, not even asking them, knowing already they didn't really want to choose. They knew it would be tasteless.

He sat alone at the table next to them, staring at the menu on the wall. Then he realized that he forgot to ask Gran, as he called her instead of Teacher, what she wanted for lunch. He went to her. Rita and Roberta looked around the room and then at each other, waiting unhopefully. Rita's eye landed on the young man at the near table and soon, he walked over and started a conversation.

"You must be hungry, little girl." Roberta wondered why he didn't include her. He was staring at Rita. "I could buy you an ice cream. What kind do you like?" He listed them. "I like the chocolate, little one." He was offering her help in choosing. "Come with me." Rita's face was glistening: "Yes, yes, I . . ." Suddenly the young man was pulled away. The girls stared in surprise and horror. Their father had him by the collar, pulling him to the door. "You fly boy, don't you ever. . ." they heard. Then they were quiet, deep in consternation. Roberta asked, "Rita?" and she knowingly answered, "A fly boy is someone from the air force base, Laredo Air Force Base. I have heard that those boys are not to be trusted." They peeked out the windows to see their father pull the boy into the side alley. Then they were statues, totally still. They were glad they were the only patrons of the café.

After a spell, their father returned, red faced, huffing, anger spilling out from his clenched fists. "Girls, it wasn't your fault. But don't ever talk to a stranger, ever, ever, ever. I don't like to do what I did, but I had to." "Daddy, why?" Rita ventured. "Boys like that have evil ideas," he paused, unsure how to go on. "Your mother would have taught you these things. Now it is up to me—and Gran." They got from his manner that it was a pitiful thing that this job was left to the two of them. They felt afraid; maybe the job would never be taken care of.

Daddy said, "Let's just get something to eat down at the parade. I'll get your grandmother." Left alone again, they were anxious until he returned and they all walked solemnly to the festivities. They walked by Los Zapatos, a shoe store where they didn't shop; Teacher had told them it was the Mexican shoe store. Roberta liked some of the shoes in the window, the shiny colored patent leather ones. Outside was the scene that often greeted them there but today it seemed scary. A dozen or so Mexican women all in black seated themselves in a circle on the pavement around the separate glassed-in display in the middle of the storefront. Daddy told them that they would wear black for the rest of their lives and that they were widows, sitting together to beg. Rita looked away, trying not to let them catch her eye. Florinda had told her that some of them would try to put the evil eye on you if you don't give them money and she didn't need any more bad luck.

Suddenly color was everywhere. On the faces, on the clothes, on the vendor treats, the sky, the floats, the mariachi bands. The memories flooded back of the other years. They were clear and good. Red and white serapes, pure blue sky, pink cotton candy, the colorful tin store signs, the shiny beaded décor of the musicians' outfits. They had been here with her and now they must try to enjoy this Mexican-Texan celebration without her. All of them lightened, smiled and Rita and Roberta giggled at the clowns preceding the parade.

And then came the floats. Each one with two or three beautiful girls in bead laden satin gowns, the most beautiful ruffled things they had ever seen. Teacher said, "There are at least ten or more fancy dress balls for the upper class of Laredo and each dress is said to cost upward of ten thousand dollars." The floats were covered with the real flowers, a bed of them for the beautiful women.

They ate cabrito sandwiches from a nearby stand. Afterward Daddy said it was goat meat. Rita was disgusted but Roberta was intrigued. With the spicy taste in their mouths, they went on to the Mexican candy, cajetas, delicious and soothing, soft and runny in cardboard cartons.

Smells surrounded them—spices, dust, sweat, perfume, and urine from the many portable johns. And there was noise everywhere—music coming from various openings: conjunto bands, mariachi bands, singers, hawkers yelling, and loudspeaker announcements. Then the military bands—lots of horn sounds.

They finally sat on bleachers, watching the parade, squeezed together while listening to the ahs and ohs and the clapping and whistling. They saw Princess Pocahontas and thought of her saving John Smith, whom they hoped was their relative. Her outfit was beautiful reds and yellows and purples with feathers sprouting out of her head. She was Roberta's favorite. They didn't join in the clapping and oohing. They sat quietly, Rita and Roberta leaning into each other.

Finally Teacher said, "Bob, this is enough. Let's beat the crowds home."

Roberta was ready. They'd had confetti thrown on them in bagfuls and they wanted out of the noise and dust and bodies. As they headed to the car, a large Mexican woman in black stopped right in front of Roberta who knew what was coming. The woman's hand reached out *"Ché chulo."* She squeezed Roberta's chin. The girls have learned that when a Mexican widow gave a compliment they must touch the receiver or it would bring bad luck. Still, it scared Roberta that a stranger had reached out to touch her face.

"It is much too hot to go home." Daddy announced as they neared the downtown area. They knew what is coming, and were now revived and full of anticipation. "Let's see what's on at the movies." They often did this after a shopping trip to Laredo— watch some movie, any movie, to wait to drive home when things cooled down.

As they entered the main plaza, the one with the City Hall and Laredo Public Library on top, Teacher pointed. "Look Bob, *Gone with the Wind* is playing at the Plaza Theater." She preferred the Plaza. She thought it was for Anglos and the Tivoli was for Mexicans. Was it?

"It won't be crowded. Everyone is at the parade," Rita announced. But for once, she was wrong. They couldn't get four seats together so Daddy found two for the girls down front and headed to sit with their grandmother in the back.

There was one seat to the left of Roberta. A couple came in and the woman, who followed a very large man, sat in it. He came right on over and plopped right down on top of Roberta. She had no idea what to do so she remained silent. She tried to get Rita's attention by making faces but she heard the previews starting and Rita who read movie magazines constantly, was enthralled in the screen. Roberta sat very still. It never occurred to her that if she moved or poked him, she could get his attention. She was a child. She couldn't bother an adult.

Finally, after what seemed like an eternity, his wife said in the sweetest voice, "Honey, I think you are sitting on a little girl." He wiggled, turns around where he could see her, and said, "Oh, you are so little and it is so dark." They both got up and moved out of that aisle.

Rita put her arm around Roberta. "Are you okay?" She asked twice but Roberta didn't know how to answer. She was physically okay. But was she now so insignificant from life's events that no one saw or felt her presence? If so, who would watch over her? Maybe Rita.

On the ride home, Rita had not drawn the line down the middle of the back seat as she was wont to do. Instead she leaned into her sister to protect her. Night came down, bringing with it the *Louisiana Hayride* on the radio straight from Shreveport, Louisiana. They all knew that our grandmother hated it but she didn't say a word. She knew when their mother was alive it was and still was a ritual, maybe bringing more comfort now than ever before. The girls see the lights from the radio and hear Lefty Frizell singing, "I Want to be with You Always."

Eighteen
The Robbery
1956

"I WOULD NOT aim to kill your boys," Reta Ingersoll pronounced flat out. "But I would aim to maim them. I'd try for their legs. Mister, your sons are like Fagan's boys, flitting around the neighborhood like a flock of wild-winged blackbirds, taking whatever they see fit, anything that isn't tied down."

Reta Ingersoll had prepared her soliloquy for two days, sitting in her rocker on the front porch, holding her rifle frontier style across her lap. She was glad that her porch was screened in, surrounded by oleander bushes, as she was not intending to frighten her neighbors, just this unruly pack of males. She well knew that her Dickens reference might be lost on him, but with his long hair and scrawny face, he did resemble Fagan. His boys were as rag tattered as those boys she'd read about long ago, in high school in Nebraska City. "Long ago," she said right out loud. The picture that festered in her mind was a long, narrow grey house, which she imagined held a long table like in Dickens' novel, where the boys and their wifeless father sat to plan their thievery.

It turned out to be true.

Her house had been robbed while she was on vacation in Leakey, Texas, with her granddaughters and son-in-law. She now walked up the road to her neighbor's house, her speech in tow. "Now, Mister, I want you to give me back everything your sons robbed from me by tomorrow evening." When he invited her in, she sniffed and declined. "No, I won't enter a den of thieves." She continued her speech on the stoop of the narrow house, although she could see the long table of deceit through the doorway.

"If you don't comply, I will have to confer with the sheriff." She almost choked on her own words, as she knew well that the sheriff might be useless, but she also knew that invoking authority was the right way to proceed.

Their father turned to admonish his boys. "You no-good rapscallions, how many times have I told you . . . ?" He cuffed them about the head. This behavior upset Reta more than she expected. She interrupted. "This physical punishment isn't necessary. I am fully aware that you are complicit in the crime with your sons. And high school boys walking home from school found my diamond rings scattered on the ground by the railroad. The very rings that Mr. Ingersoll himself gifted me before his passing."

Sherriff Martinez had stopped at her house with a report. "Some teenagers walking by the train tracks noticed shiny things, thrown all about by the main crossing and when they knelt down, they saw rings scattered like flowers next to knotted up Kleenex and necklaces and earrings. They were wise enough of the world to know that it was not costume jewelry so they took it to one of their mothers who told them to go right to me."

Reta was amazed at the sheriff's long soliloquy and at his having come into possession of the things she missed the most, the adornments Bob Ingersoll had given her. She could see her things scattered about and shuddered to think they might have stayed there to be ruined by car tires, pouring rain, summer showers, mud runs, and later unaware scuffing shoes.

"But you must know he also bestowed a rifle for me to use for an occasion such as this. I will use it to frighten your boys." Then she made her speech, her maiming soliloquy. Her voice was so proper and highfalutin' that they knew he'd put on a good front by chastising his boys. Even if she thought he'd directed his sons to rob, she couldn't stand for him hitting them.

He upped the ante. "Mrs. Ingersoll, I will whip these boys within an inch of their lives."

She realized that she wanted only for the boys to regret their actions, to learn a lesson, and change their wayward ways.

She went on as though she had the upper hand, although if anyone else had been present, they would have recognized that it belonged to the boys' father. "No need. I won't press charges—only out of the goodness of her heart—if her things are in their rightful place as I've requested. Good day to you."

"And a good day to you too, madam," he said, a smile playing at his lips. Still, Reta thought that she'd won the day and excused his jocular manner to his being raised mostly on his own, probably motherless like his wild pack of coyotes.

As she walked back up the road to her own home, she called out to her dead husband, "Bob, I know you didn't know we'd be surrounded when you built our lovely home south of the railroad tracks. Who knew we'd end up in the Mexican part of town. I know you wouldn't have wanted your widow to live here alone. Even though I champion education for these folks, I don't have to fraternize with them. But I must tell you that I did tell a little white lie when I told that man that you gave me that rusty rifle for protection. I know you just left it there when you exited without warning. Probably, you would have thrown it away on that Tuesday if you'd known that Wednesday would be your last one on earth. Although I am getting on in years, I have enough of a right mind to know the rifle is useless. But they don't know that, and they don't need to know it. I'll protect our place with her last breath. Oh, and I wish you could have seen the lilacs this year. They take a person's breath away, her dear." At the conclusion of her heavenly conversation, she rushed into the house, her enclave against this neighborhood, put the rifle back in its rightful place, and turned to making supper. While she cooked, she came to the realization that she should take up Bob Smith's offer of her taking care of the girls. She would be able to be a better caretaker than he. She would just move her house, kit and caboodle, to the right side of Mirando City. They would all live together there.

ROBERTA, NOW IN third grade, had noticed on the first day of school, a quiet, intelligent boy who sat behind her in the row. Frank, one of the brothers, didn't seem a roughhouse type, as most of the other boys did. In fact, her teacher had assigned them to work on a project together, and she knew that her teacher understood her shyness, so would not have put her in with a scoundrel. They worked on building a little fort for some historical reason that had escaped them. They quietly had fun with their creation, which Frank said looked more like a chicken coop than a fort. They'd laughed together at that thought.

Her family had come home from a vacation to Leakey to find her grandmother's house vandalized, her property strewn about or missing. She had been unable to believe that Frank could have a part in this but he missed two days of school after his family's hand in it came to light. The day he returned, he didn't come to the seat behind her, but after talking with Mr. Helwig, he was allowed to stand at the table in the back of the room. She winced at the thought that at home he'd been whipped severely because that's where the boys went after a paddling by the principal for misdeeds.

Later, when they were getting ready for lunch, Frank came to her desk as she put away her tablet, pen, and ink bottle. Head down, he made one statement, never looking at her. "I stayed outside because I couldn't go in." Although the words weren't an apology for his family's actions, she knew he'd drawn a line for her. He knew that Mrs. Ingersoll was her grandmother, and he couldn't steal from her. She was quietly pleased and looked at him until he looked back, when she gave him a little smile. He looked at her with sadness. She hopped out to meet her girlfriends, keeping her knowledge to herself. Even to their questions, "Did Frank rob your grandmother? Is he a thief?" she simply answered, "No, and I don't want to talk about it." When they kept pushing at her with questions, she scooted down to a different part of the sidewalk to eat her bag lunch. Although she didn't have the nerve to tell them off, she was silent. That night her father reported that almost everything that was missing had appeared on Reta Ingersoll's front porch.

Nineteen
Much Obliged
1958

"WHAT IS THAT? *¿Qué estoy viendo?* Juan? Mary mother of Jesus!" On Mother's Day, a burning hot Sunday after lunch, two friends, Juan and Rofie, were out for a drive in Juan's Chevy. They drove slowly, lazily out of town. Suddenly, Juan slammed the car to a dead stop. Both boys covered their mouths in horror. A wisp of a girl, arms raised, floated toward them out of the cloud of heat sent up from the steaming pavement. Momentarily mesmerized by the ghostly vision, they failed to see for a few seconds the mangled green and white Ford Fairlane behind her, its front smashed into a bridge.

Rofie recovered first, jumped out, ran to her. He yelled back, "It's one of Bob Smith's girls." He came closer. "It's Roberta. Go get Mr. Smith."

Juan peeled his Chevy away so quickly that Rofie was stunned by the fact that he was alone with this girl. By himself, he should save her. He shuddered to realize what was ahead. Roberta's white t-shirt and pale blue short shorts were splotched red, blood ran from a deep violet gash hovering by her left eye and poured from a slit in her chin. As she reached him, he grasped her hands to stop their clawing at the air. Looking now into her eyes, he saw their vacancy. He knew she was not seeing; she was in shock.

Two years later, when he courted Roberta, holding her in his arms, she would tell him that even though she was in such a state that day, she had sensed his presence. She knew he was there to save her. He also had a strange feeling that day that he'd been on that road for a reason. He'd heard that the Chinese thought that if you saved someone's life, you were responsible for him or her forever.

Desperate and eerie wheezes filled the air—"um, aggh," sounds of gurgling blood. He understood that she couldn't breathe, and knew she must have help soon. As he guided Roberta back to the Ford, he prayed out loud. He prayed to Mary. "Holy Mary mother of God, help us now in our hour of need, make this girl whole again. I will pay penance for your miracle." He knew that he should say what the penance would be, but he was frightened to think of it just now. He placed her carefully on the ground and leaned on the uncrushed side of the Ford, thinking of what he must do. Go to the others. Four girls took rides most afternoons together. Roberta, Rita, Roberta's friend Diane, and Diane's sister Shirley.

What he found in the car was gruesome. Rita's head was thrown back, her nose broken by the steering wheel. She looked in recognition at Rofie. Next to her, Shirley was crumpled into the floorboard, blood dripping down her face. In the backseat, Diane lay moaning—the absence of blood made her seem okay, but time would reveal otherwise. Rofie quickly ascertained that Roberta needs the most immediate help. Thankfully, Juan and Mr. Smith arrived just then. Mr. Smith placed his hand firmly on the car bumper. It cooked his palm in the heat. He let it stay. The pain steadied him, helped him to know the blood, gasoline, and moaning were real.

"Oh, dear God." Bob saw the crumpled girls in the car first, then Roberta seated on the other side, on the ground. He had called an ambulance from home to take the girls to Laredo. He knew Roberta could not wait. He guided his other daughter over to Juan's car. She sat in front between Juan and Rofie. Bob carried Roberta over and held her in the back seat, leaning her head on his chest, her breathing growing even more labored. Sweat poured off Juan from the heat and the responsibility. Hearing the approaching ambulance, he drove faster than he had ever gone. It felt strange to be driving Anglo girls to the hospital. He wondered if it would be more to Mr. Smith's liking if one of the Anglo high school boys were in his place.

Rita pleaded, "Don't let Roberta die. Don't let her die."

Bob knew he must save his girls. He saw the words he wrote that Good Friday morning when Roseglen left him. "Today her Rose left Rita and Roberta in her care. I will take care of them, her Rose of San Antone."

Roseglen entrusted the girls to him at her death. He could not fail her. Juan slid the car into the Emergency Room bay at Mercy Hospital in what felt like minutes. Orderlies rushed out with stretchers. Lying on them, the girls looked up to see the sky, a brilliant blue, a sight out of place.

Blue short shorts and panties were cut up the legs and thighs to the waists. The white t-shirts slit with the bras up the front. Pieces of cloth were stripped off the girls' bodies. A mound of cloth appears bloodied on the floor. First, Roberta was taken away. Soon after, Rita. Then there was a whine outside, and the other girls appeared on stretchers.

Mr. Smith was called away by Dr. Cigarroa. "She will need surgery immediately, Mr. Smith." This doctor was Mexican and yet Bob felt that his girls were safe with him. Still he has questions that needed answers. Would his girls recover? Will the Gill girls be okay? Would he be sued for this? He was responsible for all of it. His daughter driving at a young age, her lack of driving experience. He knew it was usual to drive young in this little South Texas town, but with the carnage, he worried. Just as he thought this, the Gill girls' parents appeared. The mother, Ollie, did all of the talking. "We are here to help all of the girls. Are you okay, Bob?" She was a gorgeous brunette who had a beautiful smile. He almost smiled at her, but caught himself. He remembered where they are—in an emergency room.

He told Ollie what the doctor had told him. "Roberta is as we speak having a tracheostomy to make her able to breathe. He said he must expedite this or she would die." He felt Ollie's soft arms around him; smelled her perfume and only then he let tears run down his cheeks. He felt the fear surging like a chemical throughout his body. Then he was lying down with a nurse's soft hand on his forehead.

She leaned close to his face. "You passed out. It is to be expected. To see your daughters like that . . ."

He knew that she felt his concern. Perhaps people rarely survived such accidents.

"Hitting the back of the front seat with her neck, I was told Roberta made a V shape in the seat back," the nurse continued.

He was very glad to be lying down when he heard those words. It made him deeply tired, but he stayed awake lying there until he felt strong enough to join the others in the waiting room.

Bob wondered why he was experiencing so much near-death in his family. No one else knew that the girls' stepmother, Louise, has recently been diagnosed with liver cancer. He had not felt anger when their family doctor took him aside to tell him. He pondered the white ceiling and wondered if his lack of anger made him a target, and as he was wondering who it could be who targeted him—God or fate—the doctor appeared. Frightened by the solemn look on the doctor's face, he grabbed him by the arm. He realized he was holding the man who must save his daughters. He released him, stood up, and followed him to his office.

They looked into each other's eyes until Bob had to look away. Then he was consoled. "She is going to be okay. I put a trachea tube into her throat. Her spleen was bruised and hemorrhaging, so I had to go in to stop it. Then I learned what I did not know was that both vocal chords were split. She cannot talk."

"Good God!" Bob thought out loud. "She is already such a quiet one. After her mother's death she grew more timid. What will this do?" He thought about the fact that he had often criticized people who just "popped off," talked about nothing. He feared he had encouraged her timidity.

"Bob, I was able to sew the vocal chords together," the doctor assured "She will speak again but not for a year."

"I am thinking of all of the times that I quieted the girls down when they were only being silly."

"That is natural for a parent," Dr. Cigarroa responded. "Let me tell you about Rita. I packed her broken nose and supported it with stitches. She will need plastic surgery." Then guilt flooded Bob again. He had concentrated on his younger daughter, while he knew that Rita's fear of doctors was as painful for her as silence would be for Roberta—maybe more so.

Nurse Gloria gently guided Bob to the elevator and took him to the fourth floor of the hospital. She put him in what would be the girls' room for the next few weeks. The room was sterile and cold from the air conditioning, and the turned-down beds beckoned his daughters. Gloria went to bring him coffee. He stood at the window, staring out, and tried to make sense of a scene in the parking lot. He saw a crowd of people collected at one end. Most everyone was in their Sunday best, men in dress shirts with hats in hand, many women in church dresses with hats on their heads. They stood in the sun, talking in little groups. He could see anxiety in their bent bodies, people head to head in deep conversation. As he was wondering what had happened to cause such a mob, he began to pick out individuals. He came quickly to know, rushed out, found the stairwell, and emerged in a wave of emotion to greet his townspeople.

"Mr. Smith, what do you need? We are here for you." "Robert, here is money so you don't have to go to the bank. You will need to eat. You may want to stay here in Laredo in a motel." He was handed an envelope by a man. Women came forward. "We went to your house and we got your girls' night clothes from Mrs. Ingersoll. She is very upset, so we have women with her telling her to not to come until you know more." "I will walk the stations of the cross on her knees, Mr. Smith." "The Ladies of the Methodist church will take meals to Mrs. Ingersoll." Mr. Christian, the owner of the grocery store on the other side of town took Bob's hand. "*Es una lastima.* It's a pity, Bob. These young girls! Let me know if you need anything from her store."

This was a conglomeration of offers crossing different classes, religions, Catholic and Protestant, Mexicans and Anglos together. He felt a pride and a deep sorrow—pride that this event brought folks together and sorrow that it took such devastation to do so. He said a silent short prayer of thanks. "Lord, I am much obliged."

After many embraces and words of gratefulness, he ascended again to the room where his two girls would soon be brought to heal. For some reason, his throat filled with fear as he climbed each stair. Each footfall had a heaviness. He sensed why he felt fear; when reaching the floor, he saw a commotion outside the girls' room.

He ran to find the young man, Rofie, who helped his girls, crumpled in a nurse's arms while another nurse placed smelling salts under his nose. "He just went down when he saw her. You be careful, Mr. Smith. She looks beaten up something awful."

Without responding, he pushed into the room to face Roberta, blue and swollen, tubes in her nose and mouth, a piece of metal crossing her throat. He felt she has been battered by his permissiveness. He let Rita drive at thirteen. He spun to Rita. Breathed a sigh and sank into the chair by Rita's bed.

"I am sorry, Daddy."

"Oh, her God, no! It is me. I am the guilty one."

Rita frowned. "Daddy, you are always trying to be good to us. That is your only error." Rita comforted her father with a smile and then turned away to sleep.

Bob lay back in the recliner, a frown on his face and his hands together as in prayer. He thought, I always try to sort through the detritus, to sift out the right way to be. Maybe I use too tight of a strainer. I refine too much wanting her girls to be content, but I never want to put them in danger.

He slept fitfully through the night in that recliner, brought to the room for that purpose. He recalled how he did not leave his wife until her death, every night spent in a similar chair. He knew he had to stay, to keep the vigil. Although he had wanted to climb into the narrow bed with Roseglen, he realized that embracing her would not be a comfort. It would make her breath come shorter. He had the same fear of death for his girls now that he had for his wife then. He thought, I cannot survive the same end to this story.

Roberta wakened in the night, congested by the smothering smell of carnations. Already the room was filled with bouquets. She felt needles in her arms, the metal in her throat. She was reminded of that morning at church. Just like every Mother's Day since their mother died, Teacher had placed a carnation bouquet on the altar, six red ones and six white. The preacher announced, "The flowers this morning are from Roseglen Smith's two girls." She relived the first time, only a few weeks after her mother's death, when at the end of the sermon, the refrain of "Amazing Grace" eerily and surprisingly came floating out of a Sunday School room at the back of the church. Her grandmother stood in the door, singing, tears streaming down her face. Roberta had felt embarrassment and deep loneliness. This ritual occurred every year. She didn't know which flowers, the red or the white, were from her and which from Rita.

As a week of nights pass, Bob's body showed the weariness of a large man sleeping in a recliner. Then a night came and with it Elena, a round, beautiful young Mexican woman who was a nurse's aide and who had shown special care to Roberta.

She turned to him and said, "Mr. Smith, you are worn out. Go home so you can be strong here for your girls."

Her hands were blessings on Roberta's wracked body. Her prayers rang true. She put cream on her cool hands and rubbed Roberta's arms and legs and back. She had a healing touch. She was kind and funny and strong. In the future, Roberta would think about Elena's life. They had been so close. She made Roberta feel like a person in spite of the feeding tube and the needles in her arms. She worked the days and volunteered to be with Roberta at night. Months later they took her a gift when she wrote to Roberta of her engagement for marriage. Her family greeted the Smiths like royalty. Her daddy told her parents. "I don't know what I would have done without her. I couldn't have done it on my own."

AFTER TWO WEEKS of medical care, the two Smith girls were allowed to navigate down the hall in wheelchairs to visit the Gill girls. Diane had broken several vertebrae, so must lie flat in bed. They all stared at each other and then looked away, up at the big glass windows to an outside they had been away from for weeks. Giggled erupt. Rita, relieved, smiled broadly. Her nose hurt when she laughed, and she snorted. She had honestly thought that the close foursome might be disrupted now. But both Diane and Shirley showed them otherwise.

"We are such celebrities now!" she voiced.

"A bit famous," Diane added.

Neither Smith girl had thought of the fame this brought them. But Rita had toyed with the bad girl aspect: four very young girls ranging from eleven to fourteen driving too fast, smoking, and not paying attention.

"Now, we are the wild ones," Shirley bragged.

Roberta recognized that, while this was not her chosen goal, she did have great admiration for the independent spirit of the other three and she was glad she could not verbally agree to the new status. Maybe this was why she had been silenced. She did not like to be contrary. Still it hurt her deeply to not stand up against anything she knew was not just. Her silence did not have to be acquiescence, but it would not upset the others either. Later in life, she would come to know that speaking out against injustice was important, and it fit more with her true nature.

But in her early adolescence, that concept was muddled. Bob's concerns about a quiet girl being silenced were justified.

All three were grateful and just a tad guilty.

Shirley announced, "I am the least hurt. I have only cuts from the windshield. I will be the first to be released. I will tell our story." It was truly a tale of woe, and they did not even know yet that Rofie would walk on his knees around the Stations of the Cross in the San Augustine Cathedral in Laredo as his promised penance. It was silent now as Rita, Shirley, Roberta, and Diane fidgeted and gazed in wonder that they were a "story."

Bells, the tinkling of bells moving slowly down the hospital hallway, awakened Bob to his current reality. Checking to see if the tinkling represented death coming near, Bob slowly opened the hall door to a nun's reprimand.

"Never, never come out when the priest is going in the hall. He is giving the communion to Catholics." Admonished by a bell-ringing nun, Bob felt guilty for having interrupted a ritual and quickly withdrew, his large body shrinking in shame. Roseglen had shown him that being prejudiced against someone for religion was a form of racism. He did not want to appear to think as many did—that Catholicism was bad. This Catholic hospital would save his girls. He smiled to think of what he heard outside the room when the four girls reunited for the first time. They knew they have a story to tell. He was so very grateful that three of the girls would be able to do the telling soon—Roberta, just a little later.

Twenty

Silence
1959

AFTER THE ACCIDENT, Roberta moved into a silent state. *Silencio*. The Spanish word was stronger, more forceful than "silence." It fit her state of mind perfectly. She was very comfortable being quiet. No one told her to speak up or queried her to enter into the conversation. As a result, they were not frustrated by the one-word answers she had previously used as her barrier against conversing. Now everyone accepted her silence. It was no longer a refusal. She now had a convenient medical condition.

She possessed a wall. Her silence provided a border for her. A border between what and what you might well ask. A barrier between ideas, places, people, objects. In a discussion, she became a bookmark, a place marker. A non-participant made others pause in their goings-on. They thought she was listening more carefully and perhaps more critically. As a result, people chose their words carefully. Still, they thought that she couldn't repeat their words to others. Her mind was her only method of saving their words. Her means of communication was her magic slate where she could write her own words and others words, but its impermanence gave others a false sense of safety. The words she heard, she remembered. Living as if she were an actor in a silent movie for almost a year provided her with a venue to start searching for her real voice, for the real Roberta. She was a vessel. A repository of ideas. It was then that she formed some ideas about herself and the world. She sorted the sacred from the mundane. She divvied up personal characteristics among her friends and herself. She was creating what kind of people they were in her mind.

As an adolescent she sat on her bike at the edge of town, looking out, wishing for more, more cities, ideas, people, and opportunities. Riding her bike offered independence. The one way she showed her separation then was to listen to George Jones on KOAI from San Antonio. Everyone else listened to KTSA, the rock and roll station. She was teased for listening to the kicker station but wanted to be a rebel. Also she was trying to figure out just what was meant in George Jones' line, "I Lost Mine From a Window Up Above."

There were always seven kids on bikes. Sitting half-on, half-off. Feet dragging on the ground. Leaning on handlebars. Some kickstands down. Sun sinking. The sky becoming a cooler shade of blue-grey. It was dusk. They'd ridden in various gangs all around town, some as partners, some in trios, some alone, during the hot time right after school, through the cooling off until now. Some of them rode slowly, talking to each other. Some raced. Some rode purposefully on an errand for a parent, balancing bags in the metal baskets homeward.

They all knew who rode with whom. Patsy, Shirley, and the other Patsy rode together. Tommy Dismukes and Shorty Anderson paired up or were loners. JoBeth and Roberta, always together. There were other kids who rode regularly, but these seven were a group. There was also Felix. He was the only Mexican kid who sometimes joined them at their evening meeting place. He had a low bicycle, and he didn't participate in the conversation with the other seven. He rode around them, sort of like a mascot or an annoyance. Occasionally, he'd be riding around in a circle before the group time. Sometimes he made comments about them, not rude, just on the edge. Felix De La Cruz. Roberta liked his presence. She liked him.

She and JoBeth had a routine.

There were a few kids who never rode. Some serious guys, the guys with pocket protectors, Nolan and Corky. They didn't expect them to ride, but sometimes they'd go over to Nolan's and play pool in his garage to break up the monotony of bicycling. Roberta was always a little scared because he'd give his speech about how much his mother would charge them if they ripped the felt pool table cover. His older brother had a ducktail haircut. She was pretty sure he'd been a bike rider when he was younger, but now he was in college and was as her grandmother said, "too cool for his own good."

And then there were Rita, her sister, and Diane, her closest friend after JoBeth. They both disdained anything physical. They had obtained bikes but learned to ride them and then quickly quit them altogether, leaving them to rust in the garages. They were concerned with makeup and clothes, which biking around would have hindered. Sometimes, when Rita sat on a metal porch chair, drinking ice tea and reading a book, it made Roberta feel bad as she walked to her bike. But when she sped off, she forgot that feeling. She loved the freedom.

First, JoBeth and Roberta made a beeline to Paul's Grocery Store. They parked their bikes against the side of the red brick building and then walked in together. JoBeth retrieved two Cokes from the red box in the back, and Roberta got two bags of peanuts from the metal stand clipped full of Planters. They took them to the counter, and Mr. or Mrs. Paul wrote them up in their parents' accounts. They seemed to write purposefully slowly to delay the girls' afternoon, but they were patient, waiting for the coming sweet moment. That was sitting by their bikes, on the ground, leaning against the cool of the store's brick wall, filling the bottles with their peanuts and then eating, drinking the treat. The sweet, the salt, the liquid, the crunch—it was heaven.

By then, they felt they had recovered from the hours of schooling, and they got on their bikes and furiously headed back to the school. They weren't going to hang there. Instead, they pedaled up behind the school to a fence line, where they parked, knocked down their kickstands and climbed up on the fence. There they stood, looking out, watching the sun settle over the

Sierra Madres. They preferred to call these distant, soft mountains Wyoming. They were beautiful and grew in beauty as their color change over the fifteen or twenty minutes the girls worshipped them. They made plans. They would go to the Rockies, not the Sierras. No more of this Texas stuff. As it turned out, Roberta would eventually head west. JoBeth wouldn't.

Whatever the girls were looking at, it was awe-inspiring, and they felt it was just theirs, their mountain secret. It refreshed them for kicking around town on their bikes. Next they stood-up pedaled to each of the abandoned houses in Mirando City. They knew the ones they could explore upstairs and down. They knew which ones would be too dangerous to go upstairs in and which ones were considered to be haunted. Some they entered each day, and at some they just sat on their bikes and discussed why they were abandoned, what had happened to the people. At each house, one of them made up a different story. When they were younger, their stories were mostly fantasy. "A family of dogs lived here, and one day they had to chase wolves so they packed up and left." As they got older, the stories changed. "The coach was stepping out on his wife. She got mad and kicked him out. When she couldn't pay the bills, she left town." Stories were born from around-town gossip. It was their routine. They pedaled furiously to the next house like it was their after-school job.

Then they went back to the main street and raced from one end to the other, twice. It wasn't a long street. When they reached the end of the main street, the edge of town, they sat and stared out into the world, longing for its excitement.

Then, if Jimmy Staggs was standing at his place in front of the closed apartment building on the main street, they stopped and sat with him awhile. Jimmy was mentally challenged, and he stood here most afternoons, preaching. He preached to no audience or to anyone who cared to stop. JoBeth and Roberta sat on the steps near where he stood, not looking at him but pulling at the grass coming up between the cracks of the cement slabs or rubbing rocks to mark the cement, listening politely. He railed about hell and damnation and saving their souls. They sat there maybe five minutes, and in spite of their leaving in the middle of a sermon, Jimmy thanked them for coming. They thought he missed them if they don't come by.

By now, the sky was changing so they headed back to Roberta's street. Several of the bike riding kids lived close, so this had become the ending place. They sat there and went over the day at school. "Did you know Victor spit at Mr. Helwig in math class?" "Did he get whipped?" "I think Angie has a crush on Mike." "Someone said that Coach Simpson went over to Mrs. Johnson's for a Coke after school yesterday when Mr. Williamson was still at school." There was a span of about four or five years in their ages, so it was a good place to learn. They all felt comfortable, even with the silences, and nobody wanted to go home. Roberta sat there thinking of what was out there, outside of Mirando City. Eventually, someone's mother or her grandmother yelled for them, and slowly, one by one, they peeled off and headed home. Supper was ready.

Twenty-One

Going Across
1961

AN UNSHAVEN FACE, re-worn clothes, puffy eyes with dark, telling circles accompanied the smell coming off the sweaty teenage body. He bravely put out his hitchhiker thumb to beg all passersby for a ride home to Mirando City. Roberta's family was driving home from the weekly shopping trip to Laredo. They saw that this teenage Mexican boy had had a harsh, sleepless night.

Her face reddened. Her heart pounded. A pain rose into her stomach. She couldn't believe that her Daddy stopped.

When the car door shut, her father turned around to the boy, now in a place in the back seat beside her sister, Rita. "Have you been across?" Now Rofie's face reddened. He seemed to be making an admission. "Yes sir, Mr. Smith." Her dad shook his head, but a conspiratorial smile crossed both faces.

They continued the drive, the thirty miles home, through bleak brush country at which she stared intently. How could her two worlds have come together with such suddenness? She was looking through the mesquite trees and the prickly cactus to find a way out of this messiness. Maybe they would show her a solution to this strange predicament. She thought that, in his unkempt state, Rofie would fit better out in this desert country than in their car, with her family. She perched on the edge of her seat, willing this to be done. She never once looked his way. She stared out her window. She knew their eyes could not meet here. She puzzled as to how she could feel attraction and repulsion at once. She feared both emotions. She thought about Rofie going to pick beets in Michigan in the summers. She knew he followed the crops. This was strange and embarrassing to her.

Later, lying together in bed, she queried Rita. She was her source for all answers of life. No one else had been giving them out since their mother was dead and buried. "What was that all about with Rofie? What is 'going across'?" she asked her sister.

"Oh, Roberta." Rita was always a little perturbed and high and mighty about her sister's naïveté. Sophisticated knowledge was the venue of older sisters. "People only mean one thing when they talk about 'crossing over' in hushed tones. He'd crossed the border to Nuevo Laredo and paid money to a fallen woman for sleeping with him, having sex." Her voice belied the fact that she enjoyed giving big, shocking news. She read lots of novellas, so Roberta never knew what was fact and what was fiction. But this time she believed her sister. Her eyes filled with water. The truth saddened her.

Later in life, she would come to know that across the International Bridge to Mexico, there were prostitutes, many of them thirteen, fourteen, her age. "Going across" meant being with those girls to men on this side. The International Bridge was an architectural wonder, the first pontoon bridge to connect two countries, and very much in the news and conversations of the previous five years. She expected it to swing, but it was very steady for their car or on trips walking across it. Although the polarities of the two worlds were clear, as a young girl, she felt as safe in the colorful world of Nuevo Laredo as she did in Laredo on the U.S. side.

In the first decade of the next century, when she lived in Montana, she would hear that feeling safe in Nuevo Laredo was a thing of the past. The bridge between the two countries would eventually have altars honoring the saint of death, Santisima Muerta, announcing the drug cartel mission's support from God. These altars represented a cult side of Mexico's religious persona, not the usual altars to the everyday Catholic saints. Her sister, who would stay in Texas and teach school, was told by her students' parents, some of whom were Mexican nationals, of candles, necklaces, flowers, and paintings of skeletons sitting on the altars, adoring death. Now they were afraid to cross this long cement bridge decorated with flags from both countries. The Rio Grande below was often only a trickle, a pitiful river, a cut in the dry sand banks. And in this future time, almost no Anglos would cross either. Certainly, young girls would not be taken across. Even the border guards would advise anyone trying to go over that unless they had important business, not to cross.

The next Saturday after picking up Rofie, Rita and Roberta went across the bridge with their Daddy. They were interrogated by the border guards, who opened their car doors and poked around with batons on the floorboards and in the trunk. This was the usual procedure but it's intrusive. With air conditioning off for the stop, the air was stifling.

After making it through the examination at the border, they drove through the narrow streets of Nuevo Laredo. Roberta saw girls her age—thirteen, fourteen, fifteen—peeking out of aproned doors, doors half covered with colorful cloth, girls with looks on their faces she could not fathom. Were they looking to be rescued? Were they proud of their maturity and contribution to the family coffers? Were these the girls that Rofie went to? Had her dad ever gone to these girls? What if she were in their place? One girl's eyes met hers and seeing the chasm between them, they both looked quickly away.

They left their car in a restaurant parking lot where they would eat later. They strolled through the big colorful market, dipping their forefingers into the cartons of goat milk candy she loved, listening to the Conjunto Tex-Mex music blaring out of the speakers in the shops and into the streets. She bargained with the shopkeepers for religious medals for her collection, her own little revolt against Methodism. Rita bought some shiny bracelets.

Walking by beggars in the street with tiny starving babies took away some of the anticipation of the good food they knew awaited them. Their daddy always put coins in the hands of the beggars, who were usually women and mothers.

She loved this border town, across the bridge in Mexico. The frying meat and onion smells, the colorful pottery and religious statues and woven clothing pleased her senses. She felt the privilege of living in these two worlds, with the two countries so close. The mixture of smells added to their hunger, so they hurried to their fancy dinner at the Cadillac Bar, a high-toned restaurant where all of the Anglos came to eat. Mr. De la Garza provided a safe parking lot for his American guests. They parked here to avoid paying protection to ten-year-old boys who would "watch" your car for a fee and, rumor had it, slice your tires if you didn't pay up. If they weren't eating at the Cadillac, their daddy always paid up. The border held back people and water and customs.

Years before, when their mother was alive, they would often come here on a Sunday evening with visiting relatives. Uncle Francis, Aunt Willard, and their cousins would come from Freer, Texas. Uncle Roland and Aunt Gracie would drive over from their little ranch in the brush country near Alice. Sometimes Uncle Cullen and Aunt Ida would bring their son Wayne and join them. At some point, someone would suggest going to Mexico to eat dinner. The wives would complain, "It's too late." But someone's husband would say, "It's so close. It's a shame not to." And everyone would acquiesce.

Their cousins Catherine, Buddy, Jimmy, Wayne, and Rita and Roberta would have a grand time on these evenings, in this same restaurant. They would run up and down the dark mahogany stairs, look over the intricately curved railings at the adults, talking, laughing, eating, and drinking fancy cocktails at a long banquet table. They would periodically call for the kids all to come down. Did they ever join them for supper? Roberta just remembered getting olives and orange or lemon slices and colorful umbrellas from their drinks. She remembered their elation when mariachi players appeared at their table. They would dance around on the balcony. They were free; the adults didn't pay too much attention to them.

Tonight Mr. De la Garza greeted them warmly, telling their Daddy he would give them his best table. Maybe he remembered their large family groups. Maybe he remembered their mother. Rita loved having a nonalcoholic drink decorated with two umbrellas, the extra one because he knew she really liked them. Rita and Roberta both relished the Shrimp à la Louisianne, the specialty of the Cadillac Bar. The name sounded exotic, and the menu boasted that its recipe came from Bretonne's, a famous restaurant in New Orleans, a place they both longed to go because of the fame of its food and the Wild Tchoupitoulas dancers they'd heard about. They enjoyed the meal, served with white tablecloths, wine glasses for water, huge bouquets on side tables, soft music and dark wood walls, this eatery world seemed far from the streets.

Again, Roberta thought back to the young girl who peeked out at her. Did they share Rofie? She made Roberta think of her Mexican girlfriends. Mexicans girls knew more. At the Driscoll Hotel in Austin they put pillows between their legs and moan. Roberta asked Diane what they were doing, and tiny Josephina answered, "We are practicing sex."

Roberta took her words as the truth because they were at the state basketball tournament and she was a dynamo on the court. Flitting through larger girls like they were ferns to be pushed away, she ran up and sneaked in baskets. They were in awe of her. Roberta won in the classroom but Josephina won in public; surely that was more important. That was why they went to Austin; they were not participants in the tournaments but observers, here to learn. And still, there was another dichotomy. Their lives were full of these. The Mexican girls were shy and proper about clothing and so would not shower after practice or a basketball game. Therefore none of them did. They would finish a basketball game and put on deodorant and clean clothes, and go on out to the bleachers to watch the boys play ball. They knew the other teams talked about them.

Their Daddy was always happy to take them across for a good meal, but he warned them strongly against going there with friends despite that many teenagers their age did cross. He warned them of sudden bridge closures or requirements for smallpox vaccinations, something he knew would keep Rita, who feared all doctors, away. That kept Roberta away also, as she generally followed her older sister's bidding. They saw through their father's protective warnings but heeded his advice, going across only with him. Teacher also forbade them to go across as there were streetwalkers there. Telling them, "You don't want to consort with them."

Now, after their mother's death their grandmother, was their mother. She wanted them to have impeccable reputations. She critiqued their behavior and the way they dressed. A car would pull up to their house and they rushed to the door to Teacher's critical refrain. "Stop acting like Shanty Irish, running to the door barefoot and peeking out through the blinds. You should walk like ladies, quietly."

Then Rita and Roberta withdrew behind the colonnade bookshelf and peeked around to see who the guest would be. They listened to the chatter about tea parties, United Methodist Women's Group meetings, music events, anything coming up for socialization. After the guests left, Teacher would tell them that they had to have different standards of behavior from the rest of the girls in town. "Your mother would have wanted that. She was always an impeccable lady."

Rofie and Roberta had a sometimes romance, dancing at sock hops, talking in the school halls, and sitting in her grandmother's porch swing in the dark of Sunday evenings when her grandmother went to church. The side porch hid its face from the main street, making them believe this was their secret. Did others knew and looked away? The girls from their accident, Diane and Shirley helped to explain life to her. They let her know that she would have unbidden feelings for boys some adults would think she shouldn't like. When Rofie told her she was pretty, she was. With him was the first time she smelled a man. One day he would come cleanly shaven, washed up so that when he held her, she felt drawn in. Other times he would come unshaven, unbathed. An added attraction she felt for the first time.

The previous summer at Methodist Encampment in the hill country, she told a girl that she met from Dallas that her boyfriend was away in Montana. In truth, he was shearing sheep, but she left that detail out, along with his name, which would let her know he was Mexican. Was it shame or wanting to fit in? This was an exciting summer, the summer of the Democratic National Convention. The Mexicans in her hometown were excited that a Catholic was running for president. One of the old men who perched daily on the bench outside of Lala's Mexican Café in Mirando called out to anyone passing by, "Kennedy will win. *Mucho Catalicos!*" She felt a change in the country.

Would the lines between nationalities, races, and religious groups begin to blur? At camp, she was emboldened to discuss her boyfriend's situation with a young preacher whom all the girls adored, some for his faith and more for his good looks. One evening, she found herself walking alone by the camp church. Poking her head in, she saw that the youthful reverend was alone. He greeted her warmly, and she said, "I'd like to talk with you." They sat in the front pew, a soft light streaming in from a stained glass window behind the pulpit. "Reverend Johnson," she began, "something is weighing on my mind, and the nomination of John Kennedy last night, which was announced at breakfast, Kennedy, a Catholic, has made me think that perhaps people will come to think of my situation differently."

"Tell me about your 'situation,' Roberta," he offered kindly.

"Well, I live in Mirando City, south of San Antonio, near Mexico. I like a Mexican boy, but our preacher has preached against Anglos and Mexicans fraternizing, as he calls it. Rofie is a good boy. I have begun to wonder what God would think. Would God want us to think less of someone because they are different, Mexican or Catholic?"

He was quiet for a long while and then turned to her. His eyes were narrow. They weren't as kind as they had been when he'd invited her in.

"Roberta, there are some things that we cannot question in religion. Religions have to go along with the practices of the good people in their congregation. Do you know what mores are?"

She admitted she had no idea.

"They are the accepted customs of a social group. Without these, religion couldn't move forward. We can't follow all of the guidelines of the Bible of old. It is outdated. So communities forge their own rules. Your hometown—and I am assuming, tell me if I am wrong—has decided that Anglos and Mexicans cannot date so that Anglos won't cross into a world which is foreign, unknown, where they might make the wrong choices. Is this making sense to you?"

She would never tell a preacher, much less an adult, that he or she wasn't making sense, but she did say, "Are you saying that God thinks that Mexicans are not as good as Anglos?"

"No, Roberta, I would never say that God thinks that. To Him all people are equal. But I do think He wants people to obey the customs of their communities so that they can be good Christians. There are many ways that people could go astray without their communities guiding their morals. You are in a difficult situation, but I know you will do what God wants."

As she walked the dark path from the chapel down the hill, past the river to the cabins, head down, the elation she had felt over the national event, which she thought would help her situation, help all of us, was gone. She felt deeply unhappy to think that a preacher had found her immoral. She believed that what she was doing, even though it was hard for her to do on the sly, was the correct thing. She believed that God wanted people to judge others on things different from color or nationalities. Maybe it should be on what kind of people they were. Tears streamed down her face. She had never considered telling her grandmother and her father. To know that would only add to the pain in their lives. She knew they wanted to live by the rules of the community. It was scary to think that a preacher could be wrong. She'd never approached her Methodist minister at home because she knew what he would say. Now she'd heard it from a young preacher. She knew she was alone in her thinking but maybe she was not right. She didn't stand up to her family or her community. She hid in the shadows.

That Sunday evening back at home, she met Rofie in the darkness of that side porch of Reta Ingersoll's house. The smell of oleander bushes and brush fires came across the nearby field and added excitement to the purple twilight. This was the house where her sister and she had lived since their mother's death. After that horrible time, they both feel they had crossed over into an unknown world, a world where they had to figure out life on their own. They had no more Saturdays with their mother reading poetry or showing them art prints. On this side of her death, they had to squeeze out meaning for themselves.

They sat close; her blue cotton skirt lightly touching his blue jeaned leg. She told Rofie of their trip across to Mexico. Then she bravely asked him about his "crossing." "What do you do with those girls? Why do you go with them when I am yours?"

"*Mi Tehana*, that is the red light district of Nuevo Laredo," he said. Somehow his term of endearment, connecting Texas and Mexico, made her feel partially responsible for his actions. "I respect you. But I have needs you can't meet."

"You are just a boy; not a man," she responded.

And as though in answer, he took her in his arms and sprinkled her neck and face with kisses. She accepted that reasoning and asked if there were really red lights.

"Yes, that is how men know where to go," he told her, laughing.

She knew there were worlds he wouldn't let her cross into. She stared out at the hollyhock bushes, the porch lights decorating the side yard, trying to sort him out, his feelings for her and hers for him.

Twenty-Two

Familia di Antonio
1962

AFTER SHE SPENT afternoons with Lucy and her family, Roberta thought of her family as outside the norm, with no mother for all these years. What did mothers and daughters discuss? What secrets were imparted? The warmth in Lucy's family was different. Lucy's mother talked with her. "Get in here, girl. Tell me what you've been up to. Your life is always the best!" She said it with glee and an acceptance Roberta didn't get at home. Teacher often said, "Why can't you be like so and so?"

At school, Roberta learned that Mexican families might take in someone else's child to help a family in difficulty out. Later in life, she would hear the incorrect notion that sometimes Mexican families in poverty used children as barter. A child for a car. A baby for a washing machine. A fear roiled in her stomach. She remembered when Patsy's mother had wanted to take Rita and her in after their mother's death.

In ninth grade, she learned something new about that practice when Antonio came to town. Rumors buzzed around their little schoolhouse.

Mirando High School looked like the Alamo. The wooden floors, trophy case, offices, and locker area resembled those of a large school. There were actually only four classrooms through which the classes rotated and a library. The gymnasium and the auditorium had been added later as separate buildings. When classes changed, students yelled, "How are ya?" "Where are you going to lunch?" They saw the whole student body pass by in seconds.

Antonio was coming from San Antonio to our school . . . He would live with his aunt . . . She would be his mother . . . He was on the lam from the law . . . He was a good boy gone bad . . . He was wild, like a coyote . . . He was part of a gang in the big city of San Antonio . . . He was a pachuco and he had the marks to show it . . . His aunt would be paid in some way.

He arrived. Although it was perfectly easy to pick him out in a high school of thirty-five students, kids poked each other in the ribs with a nudge to point out the new boy. Roberta had the privilege of working in the office for Principal Peña, their first Mexican principal, during her last hour of school. She met Antonio on his first day. She wore a short straight skirt, white starched blouse with bobby sox, and loafers. Her hair was, of course, in a ponytail. She was one of the first to see the hand.

Rofie often dropped by the school office on the pretense of looking for the coach during her late afternoons there.

"What is a pachuco?" she asked him.

"A pachuco is a member of a Mexican gang." He drew a cross on his hand in the crevice between his thumb and forefinger. He added two dots by each crossing end. He drew with Mr. Pena's ballpoint pen. She made sure to return it to the penholder before she stared at the drawing. "Look at the hand and count the dots. How many murders do you see?" She saw eight dots. Eight murders. "I must go wash this off. I am not a murderer," Rofie announced and he left.

That first afternoon when Antonio came with his aunt to the office to enroll, Roberta heard them come in, the taps on his shoes announcing their visit. She asked them to sit in the orange plastic chairs for visitors. She hoped Mr. Pena would return quickly. She made several passes by the visitors, carefully looking for Antonio to display the hand. Finally, he did. Maybe it was on purpose, but when she looked at his face to see if it was, he smiled a beautiful smile. She counted the dots. There are five.

"Five deaths," she thought. "He doesn't fit my idea of a killer." He was a tall, handsome boy with wide brown eyes and gently soft lips on his long face.

Eventually Mr. Pena walked in and took Antonio and his aunt into his office. The next day in biology, Mr. Venecia, who always knew and acknowledged what was going on, told his classes, "We have a new student in our school. Don't listen to all of the noisy gossip. Give him a chance. Don't draw a line against him."

Roberta thought about what giving him a chance would mean. His smile told her that Sevé, as the boys called him, must have had a reason if he hurt anyone. God wanted everyone to forgive, as he did. Mr. Venecia wanted the students not to listen to the gossip. She would not judge him.

Because he'd missed quite a bit of school when the courts were weighing the decision of jail or moving to South Texas, he would come to the office for the last hour to work on school material he had missed. The other boys were practicing sports and he was not allowed to participate. The basketball coach was sad because Sevé was tall.

One day, Mr. Peña told him, "When I am out of the office, Roberta could help you. She is only a freshman, but she's smart at schoolwork. Let her help."

She blushed. He didn't think she was smart at life, but at least he gave her credit for school learning. She thought then that maybe Mexicans were smarter at life than Anglos.

The next day, when Sevé struggled with his algebra problem, he said, "Roberta, do you know algebra?"

He said Ro-ber-ta with a Spanish flair. Luckily, Mr. Venecia had moved her ahead in freshman algebra so she was able to help him balance the equation.

"You told me like a teacher," he said softly.

She looked at him with a frown. "Oh, no. I come from a family of teachers. I won't do that."

"Why? You would be good." He laughed.

She went back to her work. She thought about how she had enjoyed showing him what to do and then asked him to do another equation to see what he learned. She had thought she was too shy but maybe she shouldn't decide against teaching so soon. She looked forward to those afternoons in the office.

Some of the Anglo boys admonished her to be careful in the office with Antonio. "No one knows what he will do." Why should she worry? What could happen? Did they really know him?" She ignores them. She was perfectly safe.

One afternoon, she asked him if he'd killed anyone in a gang fight. He looked her in the eye. "Roberta, you don't know who kills who in a gang fight, and sometimes you don't know who dies, as death happens after. And . . ." he pulls up his shirt to reveal several scars on his stomach and chest, "I have been stabbed many times. I don't think this is the way to settle anything. I have learned."

Her friend Josephine told her that Antonio's aunt had an altar in her house to help him give up the old life in San Antonio. She had been to Josephine's house and had seen the altar her parents had set up in concern for their sons who often discussed gangs. The altar was an affair set up on a dresser with a white crocheted cloth covering several stair steps of boxes topped with candles and pictures of the boys and locks of their hair along with toys. Maybe their favorite toys when they were little. Roberta's grandmother had talked of Catholic altars being sacrilegious. They were beautiful and personal to her and she secretly wished she could have one.

She wondered what Mr. Venecia thought of altars. He was the only teacher to challenge her thinking. He showed students how to stand by their beliefs. Even the pachuco-acting boys obeyed him. He didn't yell at them like other teachers. With a smile and a strength, he simply would say, "Señor, sit down." And they obeyed.

The previous spring, the high school girls' basketball team was heading for a game in Agua Dulce. Three Mexican girls got on the bus first and took the front two seats. They sat chatting with Mr. Venecia until four Anglo girls climbed aboard.

"We want those seats," Vivian announced loudly. "Get up now. Mr. Venecia, make them. You know it is right."

"What I know," Mr. Venecia said, standing now, "is that you girls are wrong. First come, first served. Seating on school buses has nothing to do with Anglo or Mexican. Stay where you are, girls."

"Well, you are so wrong, and we won't go to the game. Mirando will lose the game. You will lose your job."

"I guess you girls haven't heard of Rosa Parks."

"Oh, yes, we have, and this isn't Alabama. You just want to let them stay there because they are Mexicans."

"You girls have a choice. Sit down behind these girls or get off the bus."

"Oh, now you are in trouble," the oldest stated and they marched off the bus. The team proceeded to Agua Dulce. I don't know who won or lost that game, but the Mexican girls won a great victory on the bus. The Anglo girls' parents supported them and went to the school board. Mr. Venecia was the spokesperson. The board supported Mr. Venecia.

The four girls' parents placed them in Ursuline Academy in Laredo. Roberta's grandmother was amused that most of the students there were Mexicans and the girls made many Mexican friends there. Maybe they learned a lesson. They returned to the Mirando school the next year.

In middle of his senior year, Antonio was allowed to go back to San Antonio. His friends told him to stay, but his aunt needed him to return to his parents. On his last day, he came by the office. He and Roberta had spent many afternoons together.

They talked about Anglos and Mexicans and the different worlds they came from. He said, "Wetta, I am pretty sure her world has more color than yours!"

She laughed and had to agree. They said goodbye with their eyes and she never saw him again. His time in Mirando opened her eyes wider to the intolerance.

Twenty-Three
The Blue Cornflower Dress
1962

"RAISE YOUR ARMS over your head," Mrs. Hoch commanded at the last fitting. She pulled the dress over Roberta's head and smoothed the bodice down her torso. She peeked at herself in the oval floor-length mirror. The beautiful blue cornflower cloth made her face glow, her brown hair shine. Mrs. Hoch, a friend of her grandmother, had offered to make her this dress for the homecoming dance. She recognized that the offer came because she didn't have a mother and she appreciated it.

She and her grandmother set off for the material store in Laredo where they spent a good deal of time picking through various bolts of cloth. As they unwind bolt after bolt, they paired colors and patterns with her pale face and arms. Finally, as the sales clerk held swaths of the unwound cloth up to her face, her grandmother decided that blue was the color. And then Roberta discovered the blue cornflower print. The feel of the high-quality cotton material melted on her hands and face. Caressing it, she knew how good it would feel on her body. She turned away and pressed her face into the mound of cloth she had loosened from its bolt. She smelled an earthy elegance in the flowers that shadowed dark on the blue background.

"I, too," she whispered secretly into the cloth, "can be earthy and elegant," and that awareness made her giggle.

Until today, the dance was an insignificant event, but now that changed. She was changing from a little girl to a teenager. She felt herself becoming desirable for the first time. She knew that because Rofie was Mexican, they couldn't enter the dance as a couple but she hoped that in the darkened gym, where they could be together for much of the evening. They spoke in hallways or at lunch, tossing thoughts back and forth.

"You're growing up, wetta. Looking pretty." Even though "wetta" meant blondie in border talk, it was used for any Anglo girl. His flirting surprised her.

"I am only a sophomore!" she responded to his friendly laugh.

"Oh, you don't know what you do to me," he offered.

She smiled slyly before returning to class.

She glanced over at her grandmother watching the fitting across the room and drinking tea. She looked excited and proud of her granddaughter. She thought, "We both have a rebellious spirit, she in her younger days marrying so young, leaving her family in Nebraska. Me with Rofie following in her footsteps."

She kept her arms up over her head, almost a ballet pose, wrists crossed; her adolescent unmuscled limbs made elegant angles in the mirror. She gave them an approving smile. She was proud and embarrassed. They were taught at church that vanity was a sin.

Watching her grandmother stare at her reflection made her think of her grandmother's honeymoon in a wagon. She often thought of that journey now that desire was part of her world. Her question, which she wouldn't dare to ask her grandmother, was whether the other brother had offered to sleep under the wagon that night, while Reta and her husband consummated their marriage in the wagon bed under the stars. Or had the other brother taken a purposefully long walk into the dark prairie. Driving in a wagon across several states seemed daring and brave. Roberta was sometimes surprised at how strict her grandmother was with her and her sister, since at an early age she'd struck out from home with two men she'd known only a short while. She thought of the lack of privacy her grandmother must have experienced in a wagon parked on an open prairie, at times with a full moon and no tree to hide behind.

She learned this about her grandmother from her daddy. Once when he was angry with his mother-in-law, he burst out with the entire story. She knew better than to ever mention this to Reta Ingersoll. She shuddered to think how she would feel knowing her sister and Roberta know her story, the truth she has pushed away.

Looking at her own image now, Roberta imagine the young Reta, not much older than she, raising her arms in this form, elbows akimbo, wrists uncrossed, as he removed her white cotton nightie. Maybe she regained that position afterwards—wrists intersecting in the moonlight, her red hair flaming.

The crossed wrists had a prisoner effect. Roberta twirled to get the full quality of her own ivory angled arms. Would her grandmother have had any idea of the sensuousness of her pose? Did the harshness of the prairie journey overwhelm her desires, making this bonding on a wedding night a duty, not an exhilaration, as Roberta supposed would happen on that occasion. And why did a prisoner effect occur to her? Was it because she felt the intersection of Anglos and Mexicans in her world of South Texas? Was it because she couldn't freely go to the dance with her Mexican love?

Her mind returned to the room. Mrs. Hoch seemed exhilarated by the beauty of the closely fit bodice, its puffy sleeves illuminating her arms. She ran her hands lightly up and down her arms and bodice, perhaps unnecessarily, although not being a seamstress, Roberta couldn't be sure. Nevertheless, she accepted the older woman's touch as a confirmation of the allure of the dress.

The night of the dance, their football team beat their main rival Bruni, another small Texas town ten miles away, 38 to 15. After the last touchdown, Roberta flowed with the crowd of girls moving onto the field to escort their boyfriends off, Mexicans with Mexicans, Anglos with Anglos. Just a few days before, she had ridden with a few girls and football players, all Anglos, on the back of someone's dad's flatbed truck to Misco Hill to retrieve wood for the bon fire at the big pep rally on Thursday night.

Rofie played right guard. He was a strong Friday night athlete. That Thursday night in the flying sparks of the bonfire, he asked her if she would "walk him off the field." She grinned at him, unsure. She'd never done this. If she was seen, would she be shunned? Would her family find out and be devastated? Reputation was her grandmother's highest priority. Now they had won.

Caught up in the exhilaration of that win, she simply slipped out of the pep squad stand and wove in with the crowd. As the townspeople streamed toward the exit, she was invisible melting into the girls striding out to the field, sure that no one saw her or witnessed him placing a grimy arm around her, planting a moist kiss on her cheek. She looked meaningfully at him before sliding out of his embrace and back into the crowd's river. She'd never been this close to the padded uniforms and helmets with huge football players streaming around her. She inhaled the smell of dirt mixed with sweat. They reached the parking lot, and the boys headed for the locker rooms, and the girls went home to change for the big night.

Walking alone into the romantically lit gym for the long-awaited dance, she clenched and unclenched her hands. She searched the room. She felt saved when, as she entered into the spirited crowd of her friends, Rofie came up behind her. He lightly took her arm. He leaned into her ear to whispered, "This is beauty." A feeling she has never experienced rippled through her body. He smelled of soap now, his black hair smoothed from the locker room shower, his grey shirt newly pressed. She smoothed her blue cornflower bodice. She followed him to the dance floor. In the darkness, she let him pull her body to his; his lips rest lightly on her cheek. He allowed her to feel captivating. He guided her pale arms to twine around his neck in that same captive pose.

Roberta

Twenty-Four
Last Chance
1962

What a friend we have in Jesus, All our sins and grief to bear! What a privilege to carry Everything to God in prayer! Oh, what peace we often forfeit, Oh, what needless pain we bear, All because we do not carry Everything to God in prayer!

Have we trials and temptations? Is there trouble anywhere? We should never be discouraged—Take it to the Lord in prayer. Can we find a friend so faithful, Who will all our sorrows share? Jesus knows our every weakness; Take it to the Lord in prayer.

Are we weak and heavy-laden, Cumbered with a load of care? Precious Savior, still our refuge—Take it to the Lord in prayer. Do thy friends despise, forsake thee? Take it to the Lord in prayer! In His arms He'll take and shield thee, Thou wilt find a solace there.

— Charles C. Converse 1868

HER RED HAIR, now flowing now with gray, lay around her shoulders. The girls and she had taken their nightly turns of combing each other's hair; sparks flying, hands smoothing, tangles dismissed. It was a ritual, the girls' bodies leaning into hers as she spread her fingers through their hair and usually Rita Glen returning the brushing for Reta Ingersoll. Although she did hug the girls occasionally, this rite provided some human contact for her; something she greatly lacked. The girls accomplished this standing around their grandmother at her end of the dining room table where she read her Bible and books and wrote letters at night.

Now alone after sending them off to bed, she quietly sang, "What a Friend We Have in Jesus," her pulled back shoulders full of pride for her own voice which was often called melodic and lovely. Certainly she also took refuge in these words. She had had her trials and temptations in life and had gone right to the Lord in prayer and he had given her solace often—not always just often.

Her hair down gave her some release, some physical knowledge that what she was about to do now was right. She realized the synchronicity in it. She had left home at seventeen and now planned to do it again—at seventy four.

When she leaned into her granddaughters, both teenagers with their own yearnings, they could not realize the aching she sometimes felt for lack of a man. She understood that most folks thought that need went away at her age. But for her it hadn't and sometimes she wondered if she was singular in holding on to that at this point in life.

She rose and went into her bedroom. She pulled the old Samsonite suitcase from under her bed. Its tan color with green and red stripes always excited her; the anticipatory feeling before a trip. Usually she would be going on a train to visit her sister Ethel in Lincoln, Nebraska or going to Leakey with Bob and the girls but tomorrow Mr. James was picking her up at seven-forty right in the middle of the evening service at the Baptist Church, the service she always attended in the evening with her girls. Their Methodist minister was itinerant and did not come to Mirando for an evening sermon. Church had been her life; now she wanted something more. The girls would see her sneak out but she would prepare them and tell them to remain until the end of the service so there wouldn't be any more interruptions.

She and Haywood James had been writing letters and talking on the phone ever since his sister had asked her if it would be okay for him to reconnect with her. He had lived in Mirando City all those many years ago. He and his now dead wife and she and Bob Ingersoll had all been friends. He called to tell her that he thought a great deal of her back then and now thought a great deal about her daily. She was surprised but honored. Their correspondence continued, deepening into a romance, and finally a proposal. He told her that he had a fine old house in Mathis, Texas and he wanted her to share it and his life with him. She'd agreed and now the time to leave was coming near. Since Rita was a senior and Roberta a sophomore she knew they would be fine. She's had plenty of time since their mother's death to school them in the upright ways of the world and she also looked forward to being free. Since she'd left her parent's house in Nebraska at seventeen, she'd always been caretaking someone—her two husbands, then her daughter, her son, and finally her granddaughters and her son-in-law. Never had she had a minute to herself, to give herself care. Now she could at least have that.

She opened the suitcase and gathered several shopping bags out of her closet. She'd bought new day clothes and of course, night clothes, since she would again be close to a man. She carefully folded the two new silk nightgowns, the new underwear, and the six dresses she'd planned to take. She imagined Haywood will buy her a trousseau for their marriage. She put her cold cream, eyebrow pencils, mascara, and lipstick into a small plastic bag she'd bought for that purpose as she didn't want to appear with too much luggage. She wanted everything to be easy, smooth, going into a new life. She admitted she was as scared as she had been those many years ago, climbing into the wagon with William and Bob Ingersoll. "But," she said aloud, "I know this will be different. This will be my new life—a different way!"

The next evening, before she and the girls walked the short half block to the Baptist Church, she suggested they sit on the front porch for a spell before they leave. Then she told them. Roberta looked at Rita and Rita looked sternly at her grandmother, not knowing what to say for quite a while. She kept talking to fill the silence.

"You girls are young ladies now and you can understand and you will be fine. You will both be in college soon and you will have your own lives and I would just be left here with your daddy. We'd better get on to church now. Oh, and you will need to tell your daddy. I couldn't." She stood and they walked silently to the church. "I'd like to sit close to the back tonight," she announced and they understood it was better for her leaving in the middle of the sermon, which would be going on when she exited. "If anyone asks you girls, just say I became ill." Going up the road and into the church with her, they didn't have a chance to talk with each other about this strange juncture in their lives; another bend coming suddenly.

The sermon was on parsimony, and stressed sharing and not hoarding wealth.

All three of them had difficulty concentrating on anything, and Reta Ingersoll did not sing the hymns tonight. She was quiet. At seven-thirty, she squeezed Rita's hand, looked over at Roberta and then slipped out of the pew and left by the back door. For a long time, Rita and Roberta just stared; they were frozen in place. The sermon ended at eight-thirty and was followed by several hymns and then the preacher began the passing of the donation plate and Rita whispered, "Let's go now. It's nine o'clock. They will be gone. We don't want to answer questions."

They walked half the way home in silence and then Rita said, "Oh, my God, can you believe this? This is the strangest thing in the world. Who is this man? We haven't even met him. She probably hasn't seen him for many, many years."

Roberta said, "What are we to do?"

"Yes, what are we to do?" Rita intoned. "She takes care of us. She cooks and cleans and washes our clothes. She must have forgotten that she hasn't taught us or allowed us to do any of this."

Roberta offered, "That was probably out of pity but what are we to do?"

Then Rita changed the tenor of their conversation. "And who is this crazy man who wants to go off with an old woman? What is wrong with him?"

"There must be something strange with him." Roberta answered. "Can you imagine? Can you imagine any of it? Romance at their ages?"

Then they were silent for the last few yards. As they passed the oleander bushes surrounding the Staggs' house next to theirs, they smelled the blossoms and then they heard it: the words to their grandmother's favorite hymn—in her own voice. They were horrified. She would have heard their unkind words.

Precious Savior, still our refuge—Take it to the Lord in prayer. Do thy friends despise, forsake thee? Take it to the Lord in prayer! In His arms He'll take and shield thee, Thou wilt find a solace there.

They froze.

"She is still there. What can we do? We can't go back. The service is over. We would look strange coming back into the midst of everyone leaving."

"What will we do?"

"Come on up, girls. Sit down here on the porch with me for a spell." She had heard them. They were stunned for several long minutes. "Now girls, come, give me solace."

They gripped each other's hands and sat on the porch swing carefully, their toes touching the porch so as not to move the swing; so it wouldn't squeak. Their grandmother was sitting on the other side of the porch in her wrought iron green porch rocker in total darkness. The rocker squeaked a little.

"Do you want me to turn on the light?" Rita asked.

"No, not now. I just want to sit in the darkness for a spell," their grandmother said.

They were clasping hands; something they rarely did now as teenagers.

Finally Teacher talked to them. "I don't I know why I was so gullible. When I think about it now, it was wrong; totally wrong for him and totally wrong for me. This man I don't really know abandoned me. He didn't show up and didn't even have the gumption to tell me he wouldn't. We don't know each other, had not seen each other for thirty years and the plan came totally out of desperation. I know you girls will be leaving me in a couple of years and then I will just be stuck here with your daddy who doesn't care about me. He just wanted me to take care of you. Who knows? Maybe he will put me out. I could be in the street!"

"No, Gran, Daddy would not do that." Rita was emphatic.

Roberta was scared. Rita had called their grandmother "Gran." Her sister was an adult. She would go to college in Corpus Christi in the autumn and Roberta would be left here to face this.

Their grandmother was quiet for a while until they heard her softly crying.

"We will take care of you. Don't worry," Rita offered.

"I know now that what I have is you girls. You are my all. You won't forget me but you won't be here. I'll be here in this godforsaken shadow of an oil town waiting. Waiting for my own death. But maybe that's better than running off with a stranger. I have my church and my ladies auxiliary. I will . . ." Her voice trailed off.

The girls and she sat in silence for a long while.

They heard a whippoorwill and then a train and then cars leaving the church.

Lights flashed through the trees surrounding their porch. Both girls feel this in their stomachs. They wished it had never happened. It felt like one more thing; one more disgraceful thing.

Finally, Teacher said, "Please don't tell your father. He doesn't need to know. Any of this." She gestured around the porch. "Please don't tell him that again I was again abandoned. This time on my own front porch!"

Twenty Five

Falcon Lake
1963

WHITE-CLOTHED TABLES with carnation centerpieces, etched bowls of mints and peanuts everywhere, and bottles of Coke piled in a red and black Coke ice chest on the food table. A sign at the door, Congratulations, Roberta: Teacher threw a graduation party for Roberta at the Hamilton Hotel in Laredo. Senior year in a small school in Texas was big, full of importance, perhaps puffed up beyond reality. Or was it a fitting celebration of one of life's signposts?

Roberta was surprised. Teacher relented. She agreed to let her invite all the girls from her class. In addition to JoBeth, She asked Josefine, Angelina, and Betty—all Mexicans. She even invited Lucy, although she was only a junior. Rita came home from college. Of course, she invited additional Anglo girls, but the mixed party was big news in Mirando. One of her friends wanted to host the party with Teacher. When she saw the guest list, she asked her grandmother, "Mrs. Ingersoll, are you sure this is something you condone? Is this right for Mirando City? I have just nominated Roberta to be a member of the Daughters of the Texas Republic!" Teacher stood strong. In the end, the lady gave in. Roberta saw her toss her head as she occasionally sniffed her objections during the event.

It was a Coke party, and each guest received miniature Coke bottles ensconced in tiny red wooden cartons. They drank Coke with tiny sandwiches and potato chips to heighten its refreshing taste. Perfect in the May Texas heat. They dressed to the hilt, sleeveless pale colored straight belted dresses with hose and low-heeled shoes. Roberta had a corsage pinned to her bodice as the guest of honor. She was loose-armed thin, almost wraith like, her brown hair pulled tight in a ponytail, her pale face made up with blue eyeliner and red lips. Teacher mentioned several times during the afternoon how proud her mother would have been. Roberta was not certain she was worthy of the attention.

Teacher taught her granddaughters that this hotel was the high-toned place to eat. The waiters wore white jackets and spoke quietly. The dining room was carpeted and there were always fresh flowers on the tables. She wanted them to believe that they were highly thought of when they ate here on their Saturday trips to Laredo. They did have to take a small hiatus one summer after Rita whistled across the quiet room for the waiter. Teacher had been horrified and set a two-month limit during which they had to eat at the Woolworth counter, the lowest of the low. Rita and Roberta loved trolling the dime store counters there and so did not mind eating at the counter where, perhaps, they were more at home.

Roberta felt a connection between her life and the life of her grandmother during that party celebrating the end of high school. At age seventeen, her grandmother had certainly "gone on," as she would soon be doing. Nowadays, her grandmother didn't seem to be much of a pioneer, Roberta was glad to know the story. This middle-aged Sunday school teacher with her graying red hair always properly pinned up in a bun was a far cry from that young girl leaving Nebraska. But that girl was still in her. And in Roberta.

Roberta was embarrassed at being celebrated because people brought her presents. Later, Teacher displayed them all out on their davenport and armchairs in the living room. Her friends came to see what she took in. The gifts were the things to take her away. They prepared her for her new life. The long coiled hair drier, the electric shaver, the photo albums, the silk underwear, nightgowns, the Samsonite makeup suitcase, single bedspreads and sheets, clock radio, makeup and perfume, all items for a successful social life in college.

This was the end of her life in Mirando City.

That fact does not occur to her that day. Although she is going away to college in Corpus Christi, where Rita is already a sophomore, she has no idea what or where she will be after that. In her real life.

But she knew she was going on, at least temporarily. That year, her senior year, had been her first year without a sister, without Rita. Her life had been defined by being Rita's sister. Teachers compared them. Her grandmother compared them. She knew she couldn't live up to Rita. Rita was larger than life for her. She knew everything about everything. Roberta was lost at first. She no longer had her source. She missed her terribly. She was her first friend. Way back in Teacher's kindergarten, they had their own language. Tommy, a classmate, told her about that years later. Only then, she realized it was true. They had a secret vocabulary in which they conversed without others knowing what they were talking about. She thought that was what sisters did. They played "Miss Holly and Miss Judy." Rita, the creator of the game, was Miss Holly, a beautiful movie star-like creature who lived a wild life. Roberta had to play Miss Judy, a spinster who minded the home but she didn't mind that role at all.

Now in senior year, without Rita, she gained freedom from her newly found aloneness. She developed feelings of recklessness. This was the first year that she was allowed to drive after the accident. Without a license, she was still illegal, but her Daddy let her drive around town after promises of safety and a great deal of begging. She gave Lucy wild rides, driving fast on the dirt roads out of town and the paved one-mile jaunt to the turnaround at Three Points Beer Joint. She felt out of control, giddy. She found the voice to yell out the window as she sped any more.

On Friday, when Daddy let her drive to school, they got out early because of the upcoming football game. She drove to Lydia's house. No one was supposed to visit Lydia. She was really Rita's friend, but Rita was in college. Lydia had tuberculosis. Roberta decided she would go.

She went right on into the little white house without knocking. She knew Lydia's parents would be working. She entered her bedroom, a room all white, sparse. Her bed had a white cotton cover, and a little white bedside table with a glass of water. And fortunately, no chairs. She stood away from her, by the door. She was propped up on two pillows, her brown hair flowing out around her head.

"Lydia, I just want to see how you are."

"Oh." She seemed surprised to have Roberta here, not necessarily happy. She looked at her warily.

Roberta knew she wonders why she has come. "I thought you might not have many visitors so I came." As Roberta was saying it, she thought this was only half true. She wanted to come because this was a daring thing to do. She wanted to see if she could face Lydia's illness.

"I'd like to offer you something," Lydia said. "There may be ice tea in the ice box in the kitchen."

"Oh, no, I don't need a thing." Roberta remembered Teacher telling them not to drink after Mexicans but that was not what kept her from drinking. She thought that she should not drink from her glass because the tuberculosis might linger there even after a washing.

Roberta asked her if she missed school.

Lydia answered, "I am surprised that I do. I really miss Mrs. Pena and the stories she has us read. You have Mrs. Pena for English?"

"Yes, and I, too, love her stories."

Then Roberta just stood there. The two of them were silent for several minutes. Then she said, "I should go now and just let you rest. Isn't that what you have to do?"

"All of the time, just rest."

Her goodbye smile was genuine. She left feeling she had done something big, not for Lydia but for her. She made a stand of some sort.

In the late spring, Roberta told her class sponsor who was her math and science teacher, Mr. Venecia, that she refused to sell candy at the basketball game. "I just don't want to."

He told her that was pouty, adding, "Don't ever talk to me like that in front of the other students. Not like a friend in front of them."

She then felt in between a kid and a grown-up. She needed to go on, beyond Mirando City, to see a bigger life. She wanted to take even more risks.

Her class had gone on their senior trip to Mexico City in early May, six students, Mr. Venecia, and his wife. They had gone to a pyramid and to Xochimilco, a lake of islands with boats of flowers outside Mexico City, the city made of islands. Many years later, she walked to Xochimilco through a poor neighborhood crowded with tin fronts and tumbling down houses, color, noise, and then suddenly found cement steps tumbling down into the seedy carnival world of the flowers. When they went with Mr. Venecia, it was far out of town, and the flowers were real. Later they were the crepe paper flowers of the cascarone Easter eggs which were magical in her childhood. Mexican women fringed rows of crepe paper and glued them to blown out eggs filled with confetti. People smashed them on each other's heads but Roberta cherished them. Kept them. Men back then in Xochimilco, Mexican men, played guitars on the boats but today the music is taped. Her class had also visited the pyramid where a woman was killed by a low flying piper cub in a sacrificial rite like those of old on the top of this tomb. Mr. Venecia showed them another world, the world of his heritage. At the pyramid they met some Mexican boys from the capital city who pulled her aside and said, "We are not the same as those boys you are traveling with. We are of Spanish origin. They are Mestizos, mixed." She began to see the world of the people she had grown up with, the Mexicans, as part of a larger history. They were not one thing. They were a mix of Spanish and Mexico and Indians. Would there be new order as they all mixed?

Now Mr. Venecia announced that the seniors would have a last field trip to Falcon Lake late that May. She was excited. Daddy had taken her and Rita there fishing several times.

BUT HER FIRST memory of that lake was a painful one. One Saturday when she was about twelve, Daddy, Rita, and Roberta had headed south. They visited the "old" town of Zapata. In a few weeks, it would be flooded by the opening of the new dam. That rush of water would create Falcon Lake, a lake crossing the border of Mexico and Texas. Daddy knew when the flooding was to occur. They stopped to eat lunch at a roadside beer joint in Bustamonte, delicious greasy tacos. Daddy discussed the upcoming flooding and how the people in Zapata were managing this upheaval with the owner, Mr. Bustamonte, his family the reason for the name of the town and the beer joint. His ancestor Pedro Jose Bustamonte was given the Las Comitas land grant in 1802.

He told them that although the people in Zapata had been bought out of their homes, they left houses that had been in families for generations. Back when this was Mexico, *Cuando esto fue en Mexico*. He said, "Mr. Smith, history will be washed away. *Disappearo!*"

They drove to the site, trawled through the abandoned streets. Daddy told them that Emiliano Zapata was a folk hero in the early part of this century, a Robin Hood character who championed the poor of Mexico. The government had been taking away parcels of land the peasants had been allowed to farm and giving them to giant landowners. He fought for their rights until he was assassinated. "Mexico is a land of opposites," he informed them. "The Catholic Church crosses into magical healing with cuanderos, the healers, because there are no doctors for the poor. There were corridos or songs created to celebrate this hero, Zapata."

"Here, here, girls. Just look. Just think, people walked away and soon all of this will be underwater. Well, I'll be, I'll just be!" Daddy shook his head at the sight of it. They saw furniture on the porches and in the houses. One house had a tile sign on its front: "Mi Casa." Roberta thought of the tiles in Saltillo. Her daddy said that people just took the necessities, food and clothes, and left everything else there. "Lots of memories, too." Rita and Roberta looked at each other with a sense of fear, fear that the water would come sooner. They were silent. They felt the eerie quality of this town, a town soon to be gone.

A little girl's bike leaned against a garage.

No one was home anywhere. "I'll bet they all skedaddled pretty quickly," Daddy said.

They agreed. They want to leave quickly, but Daddy drove slowly. Their car crawled down the streets in homage to what would soon not exist.

As they drove out, their Daddy said, "Well, that's all she wrote!"

ON FRIDAY, ALL seven seniors, with lunches, fishing poles, and bathing suits under their shorts, piled into a little snub-nosed bus. Mr. Venecia drove. They followed that same highway to Zapata, the new Zapata, a town she knew. They went there yearly to play them in basketball. At the games they gaped at the twenty year old who was famous for his basketball skills and for having played Zapata as a child in the movie, Viva Zapata.

They drove on out of town to the lake. It looked deserted. It was barren of trees; low-lying weeds thickened right up to the brown waters' shore. They drove around their side of the stretched out huge body of brown water, trying to find place a where they could push through. Mr. Venecia stopped the bus at a low lying place where they clambered out and struggled through brush up to the edge. It was dry, hot, and lonesome out there. Mr. Venecia looked worried for a few minutes and then laughed at the desolation. His whole face laughed. He broke them out of that that sad feeling. He guided them to the edge. He taught them about plants and the types of fish some students had started to reel out of the water. They stripped off their outer clothes. They swam. Being in the lake gave them a good feeling. They were protected, cool, and the water carried them. After, they rested on the bank, towels under them on the prickly weeds. It was hot. Mr. Venecia said it was over one hundred degrees. JoBeth, who was always prepared, has suntan lotion. She shared it with Roberta. She dripped with sweat, flinging it off her arms with her hand into the brush. They all did.

After a rest, they ventured out in a little motorboat that Mr. Venecia found in the brush. JoBeth asked if it is safe. He laughed, saying he would save them if necessary. They had no life jackets. Their little group piled in. Someone asked who the boat belonged to.

"Maybe it is here for people to cross over to Mexico and bring someone back, maybe someone illegal," Mr. Venecia said.

They swirled out onto the big lake, and water flew up around them from the wake. It was cool. Things were much prettier from out on the water. Maybe they didn't want their year to end their time together. Most of them had been a group since first grade. JoBeth, Josephine, Angelina, Betty, Humberto, José, and Roberta were in Mirando schools from the beginning. JoBeth was with Roberta in Teacher's kindergarten. Hector joined them at the end of their sophomore year. There were rumors that he confirmed. He was an illegal Mexican national in his twenties. He showed quickly that he had a sense of humor and gentle ways. They became friends, going together with several others in a group to their senior prom. She'd tired of inviting Anglo boys, mere acquaintances, from some nearby town since one couldn't openly date Mexicans.

They ate their bag lunches, sitting on damp towels. They were nervous. Not because of where they were but because of where they were going. They didn't want this to end. Their twelve years together. It was the closest they had ever felt to each other. They didn't say it. They just looked at each other and knew it.

Forty years later, a woman called the police from Falcon Lake, announcing that her husband had been shot in the boat they took out into the middle of that lake. A few months later seven beheaded bodies cluster its barren banks. The drug cartels were the likely culprits. This news reminded Roberta of the lake's desolation that day senior year. She could still sense the houses and bicycles and washing machines on porches rotting way down, deep under the lake.

This day, its disappointments turned around by Mr. Venecia and their group, solidified what they had together, a sense of surviving, making it. They all had conversations about their futures, nervous, unsure chats. The culture was that Mexicans stayed here and Anglos moved on to college. Humberto and Roberta talk together on the bus for most of the ride home. Classmates often ridiculed him because he and his father and brothers were javalina hunters. He wanted more than that, he told her. He and a junior boy planned to start a hunting business when his friend graduated the next year. They talked openly about how good it could be if an Anglo and a Mexican did something like that together. They expressed regret that their best conversation was taking place during one of the last times they would see each other.

That weekend, his friend died in a car accident, a common event after celebration parties at the end of the year. She thought of Humberto. His plans may have died as well.

They graduated. Her life sped up. She followed Rita to the University of Corpus Christi and then after her freshman year headed father away. At first, moving to Kansas City with Elaine, her college roommate in Corpus Christi, seemed to fulfill her wish for a wider world, the one she had yearned for on her bike as a kid. The art museum, her university classes, nighttime lectures, the shops, and the new people she met in Kansas City, Missouri. The city noises, traffic late into the night, gasoline smells, horns honking, people talking in the street below her apartment window. This wildness seemed to be the broader society she had been missing. But now she felt a desire for connections, the life one lived in a small town.

One moment stood as a turning point. Two and a half years after graduation, she was driving home down Westfield Street in Kansas City, going past the lights in the restaurant at the V in the street, passing the river, reaching a bridge to turn home. She was thinking of the art history she must study when she reached her apartment on Linwood. Suddenly, she saw a crowd of youths carrying a banner: "Get out now!" They surge over the bridge at the exact same moment that Harry Reasoner on the radio told her, "The skirmish in Vietnam is growing into a full-scale war."

She stopped her car on the bridge.

She listened to Harry. The crowd swelled, chanting the words on their banner. She was awe struck. She wanted to be a part of this speaking out. Her heart beat faster. She clenched the steering wheel. Each evening, she and her roommates debated this growing conflict. It seemed increasingly unjust to her. She felt impelled to do something. She drove the rest of the way to Linwood Street and their apartment. She parked and went by the mailboxes to grab the *Kansas City Star*. They lived on the third floor of this brick apartment building from the forties. The stairs were a dark wood their landlady, Mrs. Staggs, kept in tiptop, shiny shape. She plopped right down on the first rung of them and read voraciously. She wanted to know everything, to be informed. Then, maybe she could speak out, find her voice.

She got a job in a flower shop and met Randall there, a brilliant young black man. He challenged her thoughts and she was drawn to him. He influenced her thinking and she cared for him. They talked every evening in the back room of the flower shop where she created bouquets. She began thinking of him in romantic ways. She took him to a friend's house on a lake in Kansas. The friends were not comfortable with her choice of friend. On the last night they saw each other, he said he wasn't sure what they had together. And thus ended something that never started. But he had challenged her ways of thinking about Vietnam and love and friendship.

She began to engage with one professor after class each Tuesday and Thursday, as he gathered his notes from the podium. She had never gotten over her thrill of the classroom world, people expounding on their passions in beige corduroy jackets with brown elbow patches, piles of handwritten notes, smells of pipe smoke, rows of chairs for the penitents, the world of ideas to her. Her history professor seemed godlike. She fiddled with her hair as she attempted small talk with him. As her disdain over a large country invading a little one strengthened, she noted her professor threw out thinly veiled references of the same ilk. She was emboldened. She initiated the conversations now. As she searched for herself, her voice, she wondered what his thoughts about her were? Did he find her pretty? Or was his interest based on her sincerity? She tried to sort which one she preferred.

On a Friday, her professor announced a protest party at his house that evening. She went eagerly. She found herself climbing a hill from a busy traffic street in downtown Kansas City, to be greeted by a large rambling house with around fifty people of all sorts, sitting on the grass. In her tidy, coed knee-length skirt and white starched blouse, she was not glaringly out of place, but the uniform was bell bottoms, colorful tops, and head scarves on the women, ponytails on the men. She was sitting on grass in a sea of young people. On a microphone, a beautiful, curly-headed blonde boy begged them to stand up and "drop out." An unusual smoke spread across their heads, marijuana. She dreamily listened, wine cup in hand. The beautiful curly head convinced her that she was on the right path, the one her mind had taken. She felt a crux, a change in the country's history. And in herself. She feared for her own beliefs. Sill she knew for certain, that she must stand up.

She joined a march. Walking to the Plaza area of Kansas City, she was taken up by a band of protesters. She participated in sit-ins on campus and she campaigned for McCarthy in Lincoln, Nebraska. She watched a handsome little man, Bobby Kennedy, almost torn to bits by an admiring mob one month before his murder. She used her voice to try to convince Nebraskans how right McCarthy was for their country. She wondered if any of the people she queried at their doorsteps were her relatives. She was in Teacher's country. Elaine and she had been a part of meetings in Kansas City supporting McCarthy who stood up against this war. They went to the Kennedy rally, carrying McCarthy signs. They felt strong and proud but Kennedy was a beautiful man, making this harder. They stood at the side of the crowd, their signs held high, using their voices. Back at the motel, a young girl proudly showed them a piece of Robert Kennedy's shirt she has ripped right off his body. Was she trying to hurt? Roberta was speaking up.

Then she visited home.

She saw a difference there also, more subtle, but an underlying current of change. The events in the greater world were having an impact on Mirando City. She saw carloads of hippies on the back roads of town. When she queried her dad about the why of their presence here, he had a one-word answer, "Drugs." After his typical pause to consider his words, Daddy said, "They at first came for peyote, not the Comanches or the Kiowas, but hippies. Increasingly, every day, I hear talk of stronger drugs coming in—heroin, cocaine—drugs from South America and lots of marijuana. They can get across our borders so easily. They are not well guarded, and then there is the ferry at Meir. Only the old Mexican and his donkeys who pull the ferry, guard that crossing. Mirando is ripe and ready for drug trafficking. Your old high school buddy Carlos is a drug runner who started legally selling peyote. The money is too attractive in the illegal trade. I don't think his mother has all of her wits about her, as people say she lets him do the trade."

Roberta didn't speak about it then. Drugs were in their infancy. This would balloon into the deadly border wars. Several decades later, Carlos would be shot down in a bloody gun battle and left to rot out in the lonesome brush not far from town. Corridos, songs in Spanish about heroes, began to celebrate the cartel members.

But back then, before the violence, before houses in Mirando became drug houses, she still saw drugs as a partner of peyote, part of the quaintness of South Texas. She ranked it with Conjunto music, menudo, the soup for hangovers, and witchcraft. It would soon have a different status. But she was at home where her voice had previously been silenced, home she was more the daughter than the student protester. Lying in her bedroom, walls still chartreuse from Daddy letting Rita and her choose pink curtains clashing with the walls, oleander bushes surrounding the room, voices swirled in her head. Oleander perfume filled her nose. Would she ever be able to speak out here? Was everyone more silent at home? Her sister seemed to become even more loquacious. Were they the same people at home and in the world? Was it only people who have lived in silent states who revert to silence at home?

When she was an older woman, the cartel was strong and she read the news of the murders on Falcon Lake. She dreamed of using her voice and going home, going home to see for herself.

But in reality, she couldn't.

Twenty-Six
Lucy and Rofie
1965

ROBERTA HEARD THE pickup rumbling before she saw it. Lucy was driving. She took Roberta out through the oil fields to pastures of newly blooming cactus. They caught up; they shared.

"Roberta, Tehana, it's been a long time."

"Yes, a whole year of college for me and your very last year of high school."

"A lot's happened to me, girl, and I need your advice."

Lucy and Roberta had become friends her junior year. Most Anglo girls in their little town didn't visit the houses of Mexican girls. Roberta spent many afternoons at Lucy's house. When she'd told my grandmother where she was going, she looked dismayed but didn't say a word. Did she know that her dislike of fraternizing with Mexicans might not be Christian? Lucy and Roberta would lounge on her bed, talking about the future, their classmates, and being a Chica and a Tehana, an honor meaning a Mexican-Texan that she bestowed on me. They were proud of their unusual friendship. They'd work on homework, and sometimes Roberta would help her with her math.

Lucy would always say at some point, "You have to help the Mexican, of course."

And Roberta would answer, "No, Lu–cee!"

They'd make tortillas with Lucy's mother in their tiny kitchen. Lucy could roll out and shape a perfect circle, while her tortillas were catawampus. Roberta liked the fact that her mother pretended to like hers.

"*Que maravilloso*, chica," she'd tell her.

They'd all laugh. Sometimes her mother told Roberta stories of the Cardenas family, her in-laws. "My husband's brother and his wife are the only legal peyoteros, peyote gatherers, in South Texas," she would say with pride. "How they can do this legally is they are the only North American Indian Church in Texas. My sister-in-law, Amada Cardenas was from the first family of peyoteros living in Los Queulos, the little town near here that is nothing now. Her daddy started selling so the Indians could use peyote in their spiritual ceremonies. Amada and her husband Claudio took over the selling of peyote when her father died. Indians called her Amada of the Gardens. My brother-in-law was arrested many times until the church became legal. Many times." Roberta had heard rumors about Claudio Cardenas' arrests.

Sometimes she would take Lucy and Roberta to her Tia and Tio's house where the adults chatted on the little porch. Roberta and Lucy would walk among the peyote-drying beds, discussing what the penitentiary must have been like for her uncle, or we'd chat about springtime when the Indians would come every year, put tepees up and celebrate with peyote. She, of course, had never seen that up close. Anglos stayed away.

During those springtime visits, she'd lie in her bed, windows open, the smell of oleanders and night air coming in. She'd listen to the drumming pierced with coyote howls. She'd imagine the tepees and the dancing, seeing figures inside a circle, the firelight making them silhouettes. She was listening to something wild, untamed. She'd be awake late into those April nights. Lucy's aunt had told them that peyote was a sacrament to the Indians and that they called her "Grandmother" and South Texas "the holy land." She said, "*Esto no eta violando la ley. Se trata de un rito religioso.* It is not against the law. It is a religious ritual." Roberta thought of helping her grandmother prepare the wafers and grape juice for Holy Communion at their Methodist church. Were they both sacraments?

She thought about her two parallel worlds—the Anglo world and the Mexican world. There were two channels running through her, through Mirando, through Texas—them and us.

Roberta tried to straddle these lines, but did she succeed? Was her thinking that she should hide her feelings for Rofie to protect her grandmother and father just another form of prejudice? A lighter form of intolerance?

Some afternoons she and Lucy would go to the only café in town, Lala's, and sit on the bench outside to watch the comings and goings of the outsiders coming for peyote, the Commanches or the Kiowas. Indian men would go into the café while the women waited in the cars. Their kids roamed around the street. Lucy and Roberta checked everyone out, especially the young boys.

"Remember the beautiful seventeen-year-old Indian Chief Kick a Hole in the Sky Backwards?" Roberta admitted he hoped he would be back.

"Sure, he was so handsome, cholo," Lucy replied, and they laughed and turned red-faced.

But she and Lucy had never talked about Rofie and me. Rofie Garza had been out of high school two years now, but they'd been a couple her freshman through junior years. They'd be together when they could get away with it—in the dark of a sock hop, on the phone, and sometimes sitting on her porch on Sunday if her grandmother went to an evening church service. At the sock hops they danced to rock and roll and country western tunes. She remembered one momentous occasion when she'd been allowed to go to a different dance. She went to a Conjunto dance, the music of the South Texas Mexican people, at the American Legion Hall, the same hall where her parents had met. Mr. Venecia, her science and math teacher and mentor, had convinced the superintendent that all students should be encouraged to attend this as it was a part of their heritage. This music of the working class Mexicans of South Texas was new and beautiful to her ears. Listening to the accordion beat along with the bajo sixto, the twelve string guitar, Roberta was enthralled by the blend of Mexican and German music into beautiful polkas and waltzes that she and Rofie danced to all that night. She was not a strong dancer but the way he spun her around the floor led her to think she was. In her head, she compared the rhythmical beat of the Conjunto music with the whiny pain of country and western. She'd found a new beat.

But it was a beat from back in her memory. Sometimes when she was much younger, if they drove from Mirando to Corpus going through Kingsville, they'd see a fire in a tin barrel surrounded by men standing with instruments. Daddy liked to stop and listen. He loved accordion music. Couples would be dancing to the beat. He said, "This is the music of the people, the Mexican people." Roberta knew there were two peoples and she was drawn to the other and their music back then.

She adored Rofie, his humor, his bravery, his skill on the football field, his love for her and how protected she felt when she was with him. One night he was injured on the field when they played Agua Dulce. On the pep squad bus on the drive home, Angelina, one of his admirers, announced that she would walk on her knees for Rofie's concussion.

"*Voy a hacer penitencia por el, por Rodolfo,*" she vowed.

She would do penance for him and bloody her knees, going around the stations of the cross in a church in Mexico where it went more quickly to God. Two rows behind Roberta in the bus, she wept audibly while Roberta had to keep her sorrow to herself. How she ached for such magical superstitions in her Methodist church. How did she have the right to do this? Did he straddle two worlds as she do, periodically dating Anglo boys, Nolan, Corky, Mike, or Joe, who sneaked their arms up around the back of her chair in a movie, hoping she wouldn't notice while she kept her eyes glued to the screen. This was different courting from "*te quero mucho,*" leaning into her against the wall of her house in the dark. Did Rofie occasionally pass time with Mexican girls? She wanted to own all of the desire for the hospitalized boy.

Rofie had been that person who found Rita and Roberta when they'd crashed the car into a bridge one Sunday afternoon. He'd found her in shock walking down the road after she crawled out the window of the mangled car. He'd helped drive them to the hospital, praying for their survival. He told her a few years later that seeing her there on the road had made him think he was her savior. That grew into an attraction. At sock-hops, in the dimly lit gym, they danced to Paul Anka's "Put Your Head on Her Shoulder," and she followed that advice. Rofie was a romantic dancer, his voice in her ear a Blueberry Hill voice. He taught her desire. She had found her thrill. Roberta in his arms. His flushed face, his large embrace, his shaking voice. She slid into adolescence with his gentle push, his quiet directing. She was needed in a new way: his leaning into her, teaching her, kisses, lips, tongues, his telling her he wanted her. This was enough. It replaced some of the enormous gaps, the losses. Together they floated in the first music to speak of them and to them, rock and roll.

You're a thousand miles away but I still have your love to remember you by. Sometimes they were miles apart: him on the wrong side of the track, Roberta on the right. There was literally a train track dividing Mirando City. Anglos from Mexicans. "Daddy's Coming Home Tonight," he would croon in her ear. Did he mean when he crossed that railroad track? Back then women called their lovers "Daddy."

He'd told Lucy about Roberta recently, about Roberta and him, and she want her friend's approval.

"Rofie and I have been spending time together," Lucy offered as way of explanation. "But I gotta know how you feel about that. I won't keep on if you say no. Just say the word. He told me that you were a good girl; you didn't do what we do. I love him, but I love you more. So tell me—now—if this is okay with you and if he is a good man, or I'll stop today."

Roberta felt jealous and shocked but also powerful. Somehow an instinct that made good sense prevailed. She gave her a blessing and told her he was a strong, solid man who would protect her always. She believed he would.

Several years later, on another of her trips home from graduate school, Lucy and Rofie, now married with two babies, invite her to dinner.

"You are our first Anglo guest," Rofie offered. "We are honored."

They sat outside because of the summer heat. They ate at a little table by the railroad tracks under a mesquite tree, sharing enchiladas and beer. Their young babies were crawling on the ground. Rofie told how he spent most of his time now working in Houston because that was where the work was. They asked about what they believed was her exciting life in Kansas City.

"I feel so lonely living where no one speaks to each other and everything is so fast. I feel like a hick." They both seem disappointed in Roberta.

"Why can't you appreciate city life? You could be okay anywhere," Rofie reprimanded.

Lucy spoke of how she hated her boring life, alone with the two babies. They all worked to make themselves feel better as the beer took over and darkness came down. They reminisced about the good old days of high school.

At a Christmas many years later, all of the relatives were present during Christmas dinner at her sister's house in Corpus Christi. Rita had known of Roberta's Mexican boyfriend. Somewhere after the main course, she announced, "Roberta, your friend Rofie Garza was shot by a married woman's husband in Houston."

"Well, I'll be," her dad said in his slow South Texas drawl.

"Excuse me," Roberta muttered and slipped down the hall to a bedroom to stare in the dresser mirror for a long time. He was her first love. No one here cared about that. She search her face for answers. She held back tears. She sat on the bed alone with her feelings. Finally she washed her face. When Rofie had first said "*Te amo*" to her, it made her know she was loved outside of her family for the first time and it changed her wholly.

When she returned, the conversation has turned. She never heard any further details. She was silent for the rest of the meal, holding onto her baby Monica, leaning in to her husband. Rofie had never been a whole family topic before. The subject was now open and she didn't want that. He was hers.

For years, she imagined him lying in blood on the streets of Houston. She wondered about his death. Was it quick? Did he lie there reliving his life? She worried over Lucy and the kids. Where were they? Could Lucy make it on her own? Many years later she learned Rofie had not died in that shooting.

Lucy started e-mailing Roberta. She was divorced now, living in San Francisco and working in a school with English as a Second Language students. Her babies were grown but still living with her. She told Roberta Rofie had gone to California with her but shortly left them to go back to a woman in Texas. He had remarried.

"I like it here, Roberta. The part of San Francisco where we live is the true Mexican culture. In Mirando, we were always second-class citizens. I think you knew that."

Several months later, in her next e-mail, Lucy wrote:

"When Rofie and I were together, he often spoke of you. I know that you two cared for each other always, Roberta. That was okay with me. Rofie passed away last month. He had diabetes and hadn't taken care of himself. I took our daughter and sons to San Antonio to see him at the end in the hospital. It was very hard, but I knew I had to do it for them. He is buried next to the trailer house where his last wife still lives. There is a mesquite tree over the grave. Don't be sad, her Tehana. I'm not."

Twenty-Seven

The Sleeping Porch
1973

TOWNS FLASHED BY out the car window: Agua Dulce, where both Mirando High School girls and boys teams played basketball; Alice, where they ate in a burger joint after football games; Benavides, where the Duke of Duval, a friend of LBJ and reportedly a modern-day Robin Hood, lived; Hebbronville, the largest town near them after Laredo; Bruni, their rivals in everything sports wise and home of the Moglia girls, her first Italian connection; Oilton with Charlie Ojeda's hamburger stand; and then Three Points beer joint and the mile drive by the bridge, the scene of the accident. Finally, Mirando City, home.

Roberta was going to her grandmother's funeral, driving from Beaumont, Texas, her new home, to Laredo, where the funeral would be held at the Jackson Funeral Parlor. All of the family funerals happened there, her baby brother's, her mother's, her step-grandfather's, her stepmother's, and now Reta Ingersoll's. Daddy's would be there in a short while.

This was their first trip there with their baby for Harvey and Roberta. They arrived around three o'clock at Teacher's house, where Rita and Roberta did most of their growing up.

"Did you all drive straight through?" Daddy asked.

"Yes, of course."

"Well, I'll be. Her goodness. And look at this little one. Her hands are probably still greasy." He was in dress pants and a white shirt, obviously cleaned up from his day in the oil field, ready for the trip to the funeral home.

"You are fine," Roberta quickly answered and handed him her baby, Monica, who eyed him carefully.

"Well, would you look at that! She's smiling at me." Daddy and Roberta were both pleased. It was always Daddy bending to her since mother couldn't, picking her up, making her hot lemonade if she cried in her screened in crib with a lid. She saw one year later in Flannery O'Connor's childhood bedroom in Savannah and as she remembered, it looked like a cage. She hoped hers was to protect her, not to keep her in.

Harv and Roberta took their suitcases and baby things back into Rita's and her bedroom. Rita would sleep in the room next to it, still called Uncle Bill's room although he never returned here in their lifetimes. The house was more cluttered than she'd seen it, piles on most surfaces, dishes all over the kitchen. Daddy was used to his mother-in-law cleaning things up. She'd been in the hospital almost three weeks.

Rita arrived right on Roberta's heels. Roberta was relieved. Rita would take over, make things somehow okay.

"Alright, I think we need to get going to the funeral parlor. Can we all go in your car?"

"Yes, with the baby seat two adults can be in the back and two in front." They all piled in.

Rita sat next to Monica, held her pudgy baby hand. "Oh, you darling girl. You little sweetheart. Yes, you are so beautiful." Monica smiled appropriately. Their bond was sealed. Roberta relaxed. Monica would be comfortable with her kinfolk.

ARRIVING AT THE funeral home, Roberta looked across the street to the crumbling building that was once Mercy Hospital, a place that had shown her no mercy. She looked up to the second floor alcove windows overlooking the place where she had waited with Rita down in the plaza across from the hospital while Roseglen had slipped away. The previous night, the nuns had let them visit her for a very few minutes, breaking the rule of no children under twelve. They knew she was going. She'd been under an oxygen tent, her face out of focus in the plastic.

Rita had asked for and gotten her Jell-O dessert and talked with her. Roberta had hung back, away from the bed, only going up for a good-bye hug when instructed. She already felt deserted. Her mother was pale, only small breaths coming out now. She squeezed her shoulders with her frail right hand as she attempted to hug her through the tent. She didn't know what to do. She turned away to Rita. They walked hand in hand, away down the dark halls to go home.

The next night, Rita and Roberta sat, waiting, by the fountain in Jarvis Plaza. Juan, the driver for Mrs. Dodier, the padrone of her mother's school in Aguilares, had driven them and their grandmother to Laredo because it would be their mother's last night. Teacher had gone up to her room, but they had to wait in the park with Juan, two little girls wearing patent leather shoes and Sunday dresses on an iron bench, close, their bodies touching. At first, it was twilight, and they could look up to her room, see the light. Then darkness descended. They waited and waited.

Finally, Teacher came to gather her girls. An orderly had walked her across to them. He held her up, and she seemed to sink into his arms. He put her and the girls into the car. They rode silently home in the back seat. Roberta saw stars out the window.

Upon awakening late the next morning, Roberta was delighted to hear Daddy's voice. She knew that he would not come home without their mother. She heard Rita in the kitchen talking with Daddy and Teacher. In a few minutes, Daddy came and sat on her bed, the one he had built, the one he had painted green with his own hands. He was wringing those hands.

"Is mother home?" I said.

"Roberta, your mother is not suffering any more. The pain is gone, and she is gone. She has gone to heaven. I am here with you."

Her mother may have been without pain, but Roberta was not. She turned her ahead away from him to the wall and pulled her body in under the cover, trying to sink into the crack between the bed and the wall.

Now, years later, they were facing her mother's death.

The Jackson brothers greeted them as the old, reliably returning customers they were. "We are doing everything to make this doable, Mr. Smith. Mrs. Ingersoll is all ready, fixed. Just like always, we will have you all in a separate chapel until the service. Then when everyone is seated, we will walk you down the aisle."

Just like at their mother's funeral. So everyone could see them, see their agony, Roberta thought. She had wanted to run away, to get away from the eyes. But that day she had walked slowly, with her supports: holding Rita's hand and Daddy's hand on her shoulder. Two of their uncles held up Teacher behind them.

"Mrs. Ingersoll requested a closed casket, unusual in South Texas, but we have it in writing. Of course, you all may go visit the body. The casket is open now." He started to the chapel and they all follow. It took them hours to walk up that aisle. The three of them stared into the coffin.

Rita called the errors out. Roberta had seen them, too, but couldn't say a word.

"Her hair. It's all wrong. Who did her hair?"

Mr. Jackson addressed her father, as though he had asked the question. "Why, Dora, her hairdresser, of course. Just like she did your wife's. And just like that time, she cried the whole way through. It was very hard on her. She is retired and doesn't do hair anymore, so . . ."

Rita came back. "It won't do. Get her over here now. It has to be fixed."

It was silent until Daddy said, "Yes, Mr. Jackson, this is important to these girls. You know she practically raised them. Mrs. Ingersoll did. Please get Dora back."

"I'll need to know just what is wrong. I need the particulars."

Rita knew exactly. "Her hair is all in little curls. She looks like a housemaid, not an important woman! She always just had waves in her hair. That is what women her age did. That is what we must have."

"I'll tell her. It will be that way when we close the casket for good. You all may observe that before the service. I assure you, Mr. Smith. Now I will leave you with her."

They stood looking at Reta Ingersoll. Roberta thought even the face didn't look like hers, but she didn't want to bring it up.

Rita turned to call down the aisle. "Mr. Jackson, please take some of that rouge off also. She was not a street walker!"

"Of course not, Rita." Why did he suddenly know her name? "I will do your bidding. I want you to be happy."

Happy, Roberta wondered. How could they be that? They sat down in the front pew, close to Teacher. Roberta was thinking about Dora's beauty shop. After their mother's death, Teacher had taken them there every Saturday, where they all had their hair done. Before that, their mother washed their hair and put it in pin curls for the Saturday reading of poetry. Thinking of being at Dora's, sitting in the dark velvet-covered chair, Roberta felt the silky black of her shiny washbowl and her strong hands lowering her head back into the cut-out curve. She heard the water streaming down, the always just right temperature water, then water pulsing to warm her head. She felt her hands gently running back and forth through her hair. She was an imposing woman.

She turned to Rita. "She will make this right."

When they returned home, each of them, except baby Monica, looked done in. A day like today made them relive their mother's funeral.

"I am emotionally taxed," Rita announced "Let's take a nap."

Harvey and Monica stayed with her dad in the living room. They talked and played with Monica. She had slept in the car and was full of energy.

When Rita and Roberta went into our old bedroom, they don't lie down. They both instinctively opened drawers, closets, doors, looking at their past, looking for their past.

"Look at these old dresses," Roberta yelled from her closet.

"I have writing in these drawers that I forgot all about, some I wanted to forget about," Rita confessed at her old desk.

They pulled out scrapbooks, clothes, shoes, glasses, pictures, school annuals, and piled them on our twin chenille-covered beds. Then they ended up in the same place.

At the door to the hat closet connecting their room and the guest bedroom.

"Remember?" Rita whispered.

It was a long narrow closet filled with shelves full of hat boxes. They hesitated to open the door. They were afraid it would be empty.

Rita turned the knob and found the light switch inside. They were all there, all of Teacher's hats. She wore a hat to everything. They both knew each of the hats well. They pulled down boxes.

"This blue straw one with fruit she always wore to canasta parties." "This black velvet one with a long pheasant feather was for funerals." "We should have had her buried in it, and then we wouldn't have had the hair fiasco." Rita had put this forth.

Roberta looked at her; they both broke into laughter. It felt wrong, but also a release. They laughed until tears came out.

"Look at this one with grey netting around and a felt grey band. It is dotted with pearls." Their grandmother had worn it to parties, sometimes to weddings. "And can you believe this one with birds, birds in silk wound around the crown?"

"When did she wear it?"

"Oh, I saw her wear it to church for important meetings. When the Methodist officers came from Dallas. When we had a visiting preacher."

Then Rita found her hat. It was a small blue hat with a small bouquet of berries on its rim.

"Do you remember I liked this hat until Louise's funeral?"

"I don't recall much of our stepmother's funeral," Rita responded.

"See these bent pieces underneath? They are meant to keep the hat on one's head, but at that funeral they pinched my head, gave me a stinging headache. Teacher wouldn't let me take it off. Even when I had tears in my eyes."

"Well," Rita explained, "even at the funeral of a woman she despised for marrying Daddy, she would want us to be proper. And look, Roberta, this room reminds us that she thought hats helped to make one fit in, to be acceptable. That's mainly what she wanted in life. Why she bent and bent us, trying to make us fit in. That is why it was correct to have the Sermon on the Mount read at her service today. 'Blessed are they that hunger and seek after righteousness for they shall be filled.' That is what she did all of her live long days—hunger and seek after being upright! The letter we read today explained that to you, to me." Rita noticed something in the back of the hat closet, their grandmother's guitar. Her Hawaiian guitar she always called it and on rare occasions she played it for her granddaughters.

Now they were sitting on the floor of the hat room. A hat on each of their heads and a few held delicately in their laps. When Teacher had let them go into this room, they knew they had to examine the hats carefully and put them back into their places. It was her cache of respectability.

"That letter?" Roberta asked, knowing Rita would give her more understanding. "Essentially, the letter we got out of the safety deposit box today, written by Teacher to us, told us that the man we knew as our grandfather was not our grandfather. Daddy had told us that Teacher had left her home at seventeen with two brothers, marrying both. But she never told us. Finally, it is documented by her in writing. William Ingersoll left Teacher and her children, our mother and Uncle Bill, in Wyoming.

Deserted her. He was our grandfather, not Bob Ingersoll, the kind, gentlemanly artist we knew. We have it in writing."

Roberta spoke up. "Rita, you know we did that, too. We left them here, abandoned in Mirando City. She and Daddy living together for all those years. Can you imagine it? Those two sitting night after night, eating the supper she made for him at that white metal table in the kitchen in front of the tall kitchen cabinet. He had the oil field, and she had her church. But nothing together. Taking care of us gave them a purpose together."

"I am the one who knows this, Roberta. You went far away. I came here often and watched it, saw it disintegrate and solidify in waves. They took care of each other, sometimes in acrimonious ways. But they stayed together until the end. It's Daddy I worry about now. He is totally alone, abandoned by all of us."

Roberta wept silently now. It felt like a recrimination. She had failed. Now their daddy had no one. Roberta had gone far away. She was to blame.

"Stay here as long as you like. I will check on your daughter." Rita let Roberta have time to herself, here in the cool of their old room, a place they loved, a place dedicated to Teacher and her reputation.

ALONE, ROBERTA THOUGHT of the arrival of a telegram telling Teacher of another death, that of her son, Bill. She clearly saw that Sunday. She mulled over the story of all of them that day in 1958.

Reta Ingersoll had clicked open her dark blue leather purse and pushed her news into a deep recess before closing the clasp firmly. Her blue-veined arthritic fingers had clenched the telegram tightly as she'd read it in the early morning light. She sat for a spell, turning her diamond rings back and forth over her fingers. Then she called for her granddaughters to come sit with her at the dining room table. It was Sunday morning. Teacher was dressed in her blue silk suit with its padded shoulder jacket sporting silver buttons and a matching cloth belt. Her girdle holding her in. Nylons with seams and sturdy dark blue shoes completed her outfit. Her rounded nails were painted red. The nails were not sharp—those were for hussies. They were all ready for church.

"Your Uncle Bill is dead." Roberta looked to Rita for a reaction. If their uncle was still alive somewhere before this, Roberta wondered why they had not met him. Rita gave her a "Don't show your ignorance" look. They were teenagers and for years had looked at a photograph prominently displayed on the dining room buffet. A photograph of Alma, a beautiful woman whom their uncle could have married, with whom he could have built a normal life. All they knew was that he didn't. Their grandmother said he refused her. They both glanced slyly over at it now.

"Bill died in San Francisco. Mr. Danielly, the postmaster, got a call late last night that he would receive a telegram this morning. He brought it to me personally. He stood there on the porch, shuffling back and forth, waiting after handing it over. He said, 'I hope it isn't bad news.' All I told him was, 'He's dead, too. Her son.'" The girls knew that, as usual, their grandmother didn't want information about the family out in the community.

"He was buried in a potter's grave, a hole in the ground for the penniless. They found her address a week later in his address book next to the word 'Mother.' Only that word." She was silent for a few minutes. The girls waited, examining their hands. "Girls, he dug his grave long ago. Alma waited for him her whole life and finally died a few years ago in Corpus Christi. Died of a broken heart. I don't know what her son died of. But now I am a childless mother. You are motherless children, and I am a childless mother." They were in a camp with her, a separate society apart from everyone else. It felt full of shame and pain.

They heard a car drive up.

She stood up. 'Okay, girls, let's go to church. Mrs. Able is here."

Both girls wondered why they weren't staying home. Their uncle was dead. Shouldn't they remain home for a proper period in some kind of mourning? Shouldn't they pay him respects in some way? But they knew there would be no smothering smell of carnation bouquets at the funeral home as there had been at their mother's funeral. No funeral, in fact.

Mrs. Ingersoll led the sermon, as she always did on the Sundays when the itinerant preacher didn't come to Mirando City. This Sunday, the sermon was on Ruth. The girls saw tears in Teacher's eyes when she talked about Ruth going off with Boaz.

"Putting all of her trust in him, Ruth said, 'Entreat me not to leave thee, or to return from following after thee: for whither thou goest, I will go; and where thou lodgest, I will lodge: thy people shall be her people, and thy God her God.'" As Reta Ingersoll read these words, she was thinking of how she had put all of her trust in William Ingersoll when she was seventeen years old, and that had led her to today. Her son was lost to her forever. She wondered if the father, William Ingersoll, had had a mother like Boaz, could he have gone another way? And would that have made things different for their son, Bill?

In her sermon, she emphasized the importance of Ruth clinging to her first mother-in-law and the importance of mothers in civilizing future generations. In her heart, she felt that she had failed in that for Bill. Now she was childless. Oh, her, her tribulations, she thought. First, Roseglen's going and now Bill's. She managed to lead the congregation through the communion and the closing prayers. When her girls came up to the altar at the end of the service, they saw the despair in her eyes. They looked away up to the white cross behind her head.

At home, she didn't go as usual to the kitchen to make the traditional Sunday fried chicken dinner. She sat at the dining table, still in her jacket and Sunday clothes, holding tight to that blue purse. She didn't turn on the dining room lights; the curtains were still pulled. Her lips were pursed. Teacher at her dining room table, behind her, her lit cabinet of salt and pepper shakers.

The two girls crept around her into the kitchen where they sat waiting for their father. When he came home from his Sunday round of checking the oil pumps on the lease to make sure all is working, Daddy sat at the white metal with black nickel edges, plastic- seated chairs and the thirties kitchen cabinet behind him, now painted white.

Rita told him of the telegram. "Your Uncle Bill was a rounder, a ne'er-do-well, but he never felt any affection from his mother. A boy needs that to succeed in the affairs of life, " he said to his girls.

The girls sensed that he laid some blame on their grandmother. Their father stood up, tilted his head and looked at them a while, and then went in to Mrs. Ingersoll. "Well, I expect this is what you thought the outcome would be, Gran."

"Yes, I knew it. I just knew he would drink himself to death. I knew it. Always."

He returned to his girls. He silently made baloney sandwiches for them and carried a plate in to their grandmother. He and he girls ate without conversing. Teacher never touched her plate. He told the girls afterward, they could go to their room to play. They went solemnly and sat reading on their beds as the afternoon passed. When evening came down, they heard their dad go back.

"Gran, you didn't eat. Here's some soup. You must eat it. You must keep your strength up. We all need you."

"Lots of good I do you," she offered.

Bob Smith felt pity then. "Gran, you had a big burden, being left with your two children on your own. You did your best. And now you've taken on mine."

She looked up at him then. Those were the kindest words he'd ever given her. She ate the soup. Then the two were at their stations, their dark time places now, she, her dining room table where she wrote letters and sermons, and where she read books and her well-worn Bible and he, at the white kitchen table, where he came every early morning to have his coffee, to think and listen to the Old German give his cattle report on the San Antonio radio station. He cared not for the cattle content, but liked the soothing yet commanding voice that started his day.

SHE WONDERED IF Bill had ever wanted to come home. She had spent all those years worrying about how, if he did, he would expose himself as a murderer. She knew that she had steeled herself against that, keeping her feelings as a mother buried. She had held her reputation above motherhood.

She thought of all the tears and money and sleepless nights she'd spent when Bob Ingersoll had taken Bill with him to drill new oil wells in Lockhart, Texas. He'd given Bill a responsible job as a pumper in the field. Bob told her that Bill at first wanted to do well. But as the weeks passed, he succumbed to his old pattern, alcohol every evening and finally coming to work drunk for weeks. The day it happened, Bob had sent him home. "Go sleep it off. Come to me, not to your job, when you are sober."

Bill never came. Instead, a policeman had come to Bob, told him that Bill had killed a man with his car. He was falling down drunk. Couldn't even converse with the policemen. He was in jail.

A trial followed. For once, Bob wanted to cut him loose. He told his wife, "You have given him many chances. I have, too. But now he has cost a life, the life of a family man. I think the chances are over." Reta insisted that they hire the best lawyers. Word of this hadn't made it to South Texas, but she still wanted him to be acquitted of vehicular homicide so as to not have any chance of ruining her, their reputation. Her efforts failed. He was sentenced to a short term in prison. Her son a prisoner!

She finished the soup and got herself ready for bed. She talked to her husband, now dead ten years. "Bob, we lost our son, your brother William's son today. There is something I have admitted only to myself. And now to you. I cut him off when he went to prison. Like Rita and Roberta, he became a motherless child. I couldn't abide him, his doings. There is that tie to your mother that, when lost, leaves one tetherless. It is hard to find your way back into life then. To be abandoned like I was in Wyoming is just like losing your mother. I also lost her by leaving her. You may be the only one who will understand that I was abandoned, not just by your brother, but now again by God taking her two children."

The next Sunday when Revered Mitchell returned to the little Methodist Church, he announced that the red carnation bouquet below the altar and the white cross was in remembrance of Reta Ingersoll's only son, Bill, who had died two weeks before, alone in San Francisco, California. Reta Ingersoll had made a motherly gesture. Too late, but finally.

THIS MEMORY MADE Roberta tired. She curled up. She had clambered into this hat closet with her mother's alligator purse and her Samsonite overnight bag only weeks after her death. In 1949 four veterans from World War II had given her mother a party at the Aguilares School. They had been her students and attributed their success as young men defending their country to her. They came in full uniform and gave her that purse that day.

Today no one came to hunt Roberta down. She delved again into her intimate handbag, into the hurt. She fingered the green prescription sunglasses and gold lipstick holder she'd touched over and over. She smelled for her on the Kleenex still stuck in a side pocket. She searched through her address book, looking for the right one, the one that would take her to her grandmother. She put on the face powder from her compact, smelled the Kleenex again, replaced it all carefully, precisely anchoring her presence to this room.

Then she opened her overnight bag to find a two-piece green flowered swimsuit with a flouncy skirt. She held it up to her face, cloth to skin. She thought of the postcards she'd sent from San

Marcos where she finished her bachelor's degree in the early fifties, only one year before her death. She'd written of swimming in the San Marcos River, of going down the river in a glass bottom boat, laughing with friends, watching the fish and weeds below. She gave us glimpses of her glamorous college life, late in her life, just before she left us.

Now her grandmother had joined her in that long sleep. Roberta pictured the one time her grandmother held her baby, Monica. She thought that now her baby had come to replace her.

Bob Ingersoll and his son, Bill

Twenty-Eight
El Coyoto
2011

I USED TO be a human girl, a two-legged creature; she cannot come back except as me. Then she can wander and make sense of the place and see it all without the fear of other humans.

Mr. Venecia was the impetus for her becoming Coyote. As her high school math and science teacher, he taught her to learn by experience. When he first came to teach at Mirando High, he told her class that coyotes raised him. He said that he looked at life differently from the rest of us because he'd lived with a pack of coyotes, sleeping on the ground, hunting for food, and killing his prey. She was a believer.

Then, in one of his most inspirational lessons, he anesthetized a coyote for his seniors, to operate on in biology class. They carefully slit its abdomen open with the cold dissecting knife to delicately examine its major organs. Touching them, their warm, pulsating chambers was thrilling to Roberta. Suddenly blood shot out everywhere—on her teacher, the lab table, the floor around her. She remembered not being afraid. She knew they'd gone outside the boundaries. Although they had killed their coyote, she was sure he had traveled somewhere else in spirit. With the coyote's entrails on one side of the lab room and his heart on the other, she experienced real-life anatomy. Since Mr. Venecia was raised by coyotes, she knew she'd be content to slip into that state.

She's not an expert, so all she can tell you is that you just slide into it, obliquely. There are no rules or directions. You simply change how people see you. She had to wait until she'd made the plane trip from Montana to Texas, and then until she'd crossed South Texas from Corpus Christi to Mirando City, before actually making the change. This ability is crucial to her going home. She was driven to do that because these are her questions: Does she still have a home? Has it become a dangerous place? Was her hometown held hostage by what is happening on the border?

Finally, she was home. She decided to arrive on Sunday morning when everyone was either at church or recovering from a hangover. She parked her rental car at the post office since it would be closed. It is a little white stucco building with green trim, an empty flagpole by the front door. The post office is the center of this little town. People congregate there on weekday mornings, catching up with each other. It has good feelings hanging around it.

Then—she slides.

Crawling, greens, browns in eye range. Smelling, dirt, urine, excrement, Her fur stiff, more like hay than hair. Climbing up over a hill, sniffing. I smell no humans. I crawl onto the white cement porch. Rough, black stones rub her nose. Eyes water. Crawling down the caliche hill past an oil tank and then clambering to the top of another hill. Prairie mouse odor pulling me into the brush.

Mirando has only a few streets, all unpaved, caliche, or gravel covered. She knows that over the two hills topped with her family's first two houses, Coyote will find the third and last house she lived in. Then only a hop, skip, and a jump, and he will arrive at the school, her destination.

I know it. I want it. I stiffen, then pounce, her rear wags side to side. I grasp it with paws and her jaw. Chew meat, bones and blood, all tasty. Full for her mission, I get going, Drawn away by a male dog's urine. I desire her. Still, I can't be pulled aside. I restrain myself.

She knows the layout of her hometown, the houses that Coyote will visit. On his way to the last house she lived in, he will pass, going part way down the last hill, the Sherriff's house. He often came home drunk and would sit with his car door open, his body sleeping aslant, and feet on the ground. His hound dog howling at the coyotes serenading her, she often listened to their whining songs late into the night.

Green house. Panting. Tongue loose. Behind house, dripping water. Puddle. Drink, drink, drink. Lap water. Teeth with gristle, sinew. Comes loose. Swallow. Full again.

Down the road from that house is the final house where her family lived, the house where her sister, her father, her grandmother, and she had lived after her mother's death. The house had a porch swing where she was courted in secret by Rodolfo. Oleanders surrounded their bedroom, Rita and her. In the spring, she loved their smell. Strong in her memory is the pepper bush her father had been so proud to cultivate. Lilac bushes surrounded the backyard. The last time she saw the tin garage, many of their things were piled in there.

Cowering under bushes, odors, sweet, sharp. Stinging her eyes. Going inside. Slinking under sharp tin points, rusty brown everywhere, leaving into sunlight.

To get to the school, I will pass a long street of houses that back onto an alley. I will pass her music teacher, Mrs. Stagg's, house first, then the Harvey house, the place she learned of someone dropping dead at the Sunday dinner table. Next is Mrs. Olsen's tiny house, an old lady who cried about being alone whenever she visited, and finally Mrs. Duckworth's old rooming house, where people coming to town stayed until they located their own homes. Her dad always, said, "And she is an odd duck . . ."

Passing houses, head low, nose to the ground. Tires under crowds of shiny cars, a slew of booted feet, the smell of marijuana. Butt ends of automatic weapons. Lots of them. At many of the houses.

She wonders if I see children at play in the yards or hears mothers' calls to their offspring. Are teenagers sitting on their bikes at the ends of streets, talking, resisting going home to supper, sights and sounds Mirando had been filled with in her time? Are they gone now?

Crossing over to an alley. Panting. Lying down. Sleeping in salt cedar needles, a soft cool bed, light filtering in, smelly. Sleeping a long time.

I see her alley, her transition from the world of her school to home. An alley between rows of houses. The path is lined with salt cedar trees, trees with soft fir needles, a healthy smell. The needles fall down from both tree lines, padding the floor of the alley. The salt cedars meet in the sky above the path, creating the singular cool passage she knew of in her hometown. If she felt put down or gathered hurt feelings at school, she would walk slowly through this passage. Or she would sit down on the fallen salt cedar needles, as I am lying on them now, and she would think her way through whatever befell her.

The time Mr. Venecia told her that she couldn't talk to him as a friend when other students were around, she slunk here to sit, to cry. When her grandmother told her that she couldn't be friends with Diane because she ran around with a Mexican boy, and she knew she still would; she stood straight by a large salt cedar tree and held its trunk in an embrace, the health-filled odor of the cedar needles helped to calm her. They offered strength. Coming home through this way, she wouldn't greet her grandmother with the upset look that often led to long interrogations. Since her grandmother joined her father to raise her, she had been overly cautious for her granddaughters. She and her best friend JoBeth leisurely strolled through this alleyway many times, chewing on mesquite beans, sharing news, or plotting something they wanted to do. The feathery salt cedar filters a soft light into the alley, adding another level of comfort. She'd often lingered here in thought for a long time.

Sounds, rhythmical. Push me to a backyard. Slam. Retreat to the alley. Focus. Saunter casually to her destination. Cock her head. Look up. Alamo-like building. School. Eyes wet. Poisonous plant? No, I feel Roberta. She wants back in. This scene is too much for her, she can't stay out. She, through me, sees weeds, broken glass, ugly slashes of paint. She cries. Sick feeling. Vomit in her throat. Suddenly shape-shifting, crossing over. Sad to have to go.

I find myself sitting on the steps of her high school in the bright sun. I smooth out her skirt and massage her arms, legs, torso, and face, all of me. This feels good in the warm sunlight. It brings me back to herself. I am now present. I reach out and touch the purple cactus fruit, remembering eating it as a young child, as a dish cooked by Florinda. I gently brush the cactus thorns like a musical instrument, fully aware of the pain they could cause if I brushed up against them or fell into a patch. I rest in a soothing reverie, gazing at her old school.

Then with a sudden forcefulness, I am twirling out in the middle of the courtyard, the place where I'd spent her schooling years before leaving this town. I pirouette in a captive pose, her arms up above her head, wrists crossed. Then her arms spread out, their tips reach toward spaces I grew up in, spaces the town grew in. Her dizziness only fuels her anger; the school is closed. Drugs have given this tiny town money but their illegality has left it with no way to impart education to its children. I feel like a statue, a "moving one," something kinetic. I suddenly wish upon wish to cause that statue to exist right there in the courtyard. I want the statue to be a statement about how this had been a town where a young girl could see and possess a world outside of Mirando. I want the few children left here now, who have to get on buses to go to school in another town, to be able to walk down the treed alley, the only cool place in this South Texas town, to teachers who show them another world or this town as a home they'd want to choose.

Growing up there, I'd wanted "the other" so much. I sat on her bike at the edge of this town looking out for reality. Today, I realize there'd been a world right here, going back to the land grant times and forward through her years growing up. Could it be so now? There had been people like her grandmother, Reta Ingersoll, who had traveled here in a stagecoach and helped begin a one-room school out on an oil lease, the precursor of this campus. And it was good . . .

I plop back down on the school steps, thinking how the essence of the women in my family has shape-shifted from generation to generation. Their essence is strength, adventurousness, consciousness. Penelope Stout, the first woman in her grandmother's lineage to arrive in the New World, shipwrecked on the Jersey shore in 1640. Penelope, whose head and belly were sliced by Mohawks, hid in a tree for seven days, while her husband lay dead on the shore. She was saved by the Lenape, so she could live to found a town. She was freed by adversity to become herself. Had that happened to all of us? Is home a state of mind?

The sculpture I want to leave at the school would embody Penelope's tree, a strong trunk from which to spin, arms like branches, to point, to signify what is around us. What makes us grow into what we become?

Penelope's spirit came down through eight generations until it reached her mother. But we lived in a cake of custom, the prejudice in which people are just baked, unaware of how they live. Maybe I should have stayed in Mirando City long ago or I should stay now . . .

Instead, I stride in her human form, right down the middle of the rutted main streets of her hometown. Her strength resides in having seen this, having seen what is underneath and leaving it for good. Occasionally, I see a curtain moving aside for someone to watch her march. The only other sign of life is an occasional dog sleeping in the street. I reach the little post office and her rental car. I drive on Main Street, out of town toward Three Points, the honky-tonk café at the T at the end of the road—the road to Laredo or Corpus. I pause once, turn around and look back, and say aloud, "Coyote, what would her grandmother think of this our trip to our Mirando City? Of my crossing into you? Of my journey out of here?"

Then I drive straight on out of town, heading across a country to my other, now chosen home.

Roberta Hamburgh grew up in the fifties and sixties in Mirando City, Texas, a small oil field community near Laredo, a Mexico border town. The men in her family worked the oil field and the women were teachers. Roberta left South Texas to go to college at the University of Missouri in Kansas City.

She studied art history there and in graduate school at the University of Iowa where she was awakened by the Iowa Writer's Workshop course that she took from C.D.B. Bryan, author of *Friendly Fire*. Writing poetry and short stories became a regular part of her life. She got her master's degree in Teaching Emotionally Disturbed Children from the University of Michigan, and spent four years teaching at the University of Michigan Children's Psychiatric Hospital. Then in Montana, she taught Special Education, regular education, and spent the last eleven years as a principal.